GENESIS
OF
TRIBAL EXTREMISM
IN
TRIPURA

GENESIS OF TRIBAL EXTREMISM IN TRIPURA

Dr. SUCHINTYA BHATTACHARYYA

GYAN PUBLISHING HOUSE
New Delhi - 110002

GENESIS OF TRIBAL
EXTREMISM IN TRIPURA

ISBN : 9788121203951

Published in 2014 in India by
Gyan Publishing House
23, Ansari Road, Daryaganj,
New Delhi - 110002
Phones : 23261060, 23282060 Fax : 23285914
e-mail : books@gyanbooks.com
website : gyanbooks.com

Laser Typesetting at : Vinayak Printers, Delhi
Printed at : Salasar Imaging System, Delhi

To

My Revered Shikshā Guru

Dr. Sudhir Ranjan Das

and

Gurumātā Smt. Amiya Das

Foreword

The author is a scholar in his own right. He is erudite and has a deep understanding of political sociology and social anthropology of Tripura. He presents the ethnic mosaic of Tripura conditions as a backdrop for the analysis of the militant politics of the State.

Tripura has a total population of 20,53,058 according to 1981 Census, whereof the tribal population constitutes 28.44 per cent, their number being 5,83,920. There are 19 major tribal communities, the most populous among them being the Tripuris, who number 3,19,692, constituting a little over 50 per cent of the total tribal population. The other major tribals are Reang (85,836), Jamatia (45,487) Chakma (39,005), Halam (25,692), Mog (16,934) and Noatia (12,963). The different racial and linguistic affinities of these groups and their customs and beliefs are described in the first part of the book.

In the second chapter, the problem of immigrants versus autochthonous population is analysed. Until 1941 the tribal population constituted a little over 50 per cent of the total population in the state. But by 1981, their proportion came down to 28.45 per cent which testifies to the large scale immigration of non-tribals into Tripura. Immigration of Bengali Hindus reached its highest point in 1961 when the percentage of decadal growth reached 78.71 per cent. However, by 1981 this figure has come down to 31.91 per cent. The author says, the Bengali immigrants were welcomed in the beginning for different reasons. They came to man the administration, and they also spread their culture amongst the indigenous population. As the author avers in this section, the tribals themselves were most prone in the past to assimilate the culture of the economically advanced people. Even though there is no clear idea of the exact date of Bengali becoming the official language in Tripura, there is evidence that by about 15th century, Bengali was being used in the Tripura King's court.

The next section deals with the problems of tribal shifting cultivators and their "untold sufferings and miseries caused by large scale exploitation carried out by non-tribal infiltrators". There is an account of resettlement programmes for the Jhum cultivators. There is also a reference to the grim facts of immigrants grabbing the lands of the Jhum cultivators by paying them a nominal *nazrana* and of their life in perpetual debt and poverty. He points out how the loopholes in the Land Reforms Act of 1960 were exploited by the immigrants to rob the tribals of their lands.

The author notes that the rate of literacy in the state was about 15 per cent in 1951, and rose to about 42 per cent in 1981. But still he does not seem to be satisfied with this progress and makes the observation that "after merger, little attention was paid for spreading education". The tribals are unable to compete with the non-tribals in securing positions in the administration inspite of the Reservations. The tribals in class I posts constitute only 2.4 per cent and those in class II posts constitute 4.33 per cent. Considering the fact that the tribals constitute about 28 per cent of the total population in the state it becomes clear that they are nowhere near securing their legitimate position in the society as guaranteed by the Constitution. As the author points out "the Government's own documents admit that the Scheduled Tribes remain much of the time outside development process".

While the sixth chapter deals with several tribal uprigsings in different regions of the country, the seventh chapter focuses attention on the burning issue of the TNV insurgency and its aftermath. The author covers the tug of war between TUJS (Tripura Upajati Juba Samiti) representing the tribals on the one side, and the *Amra Bangali* representing the Bengali Hindus on the other. The TNV (Tripura National Volunteers)

Organisation came into being as the militant arm of the TUJS under the leadership of Bijoy Hrangkhawl. When the Autonomous District Council Bill of 1979 was being discussed the *Amra Bangali* raised an objection that the tribals constituting 25 per cent of the population were going to have 76 per cent of the total land in the state. On the other hand Hrangkhawl started a new organisation called Tripura Tribal National Front. He declared all people who immigrated into Tripura after 1949 as aliens.

While the Centre wanted to declare the whole State as a disturbed area, the CPI(M) Chief Minister resisted it saying that it would lead to unnecessary harrassment of innocent tribals by the army. Later, the Central Government blamed the Left Front Government for its failure to maintain law and order and declared the whole State as a disturbed area.

In the subsequent elections, the Congress-I and the TUJS together managed to obtain a majority and formed the new Government. There was a sudden change in the situation and the militants agreed to surrender. A Memorandum of Understanding was signed between the TNV and the present Government. Some of the important features of this understanding are that the surrendered militants would be rehabilitated and the TNV would give up its secessionist policy and abjure violence and all underground activities. An important aspect of the agreement was that a Constitutional amendment would be brought about to ensure that the tribals always have the number of MLAs commensurate with the proportion of their population in the state. Another important aspect was to enact necessary laws and take effective action to restore land alienated from the tribals.

In the last chapter, the author discusses several approaches towards the solution of this vexed problem. He expresses himself against any suggestion in favour of total assimilation of the tribals into the culture of the majority population of the State. He is categorical in his view that integration should not mean total assimilation, and that each tribe should be left free to retain its own culture. Apart from some general suggestions regarding the improvement of the economic lot of the tribals, he comes to the brasstacks of the problem when he states : "In Tripura, the tribal's anger against the non-tribals is persisting even today. It is to be kept in mind that such feelings cannot be removed by arms only. The antagonism against the non-tribals is the result of large scale economic exploitation by non-tribals, specially Bengali Hindus. So the solution is put to an end to all forms of exploitation".

When social groups with different cultures come into interaction with one another, there sets a process in which there is mutual give and take, and items of culture passed from one group to the other—though more so in one direction than the other. Anthropologists have called this process acculturation. When the relations between the groups are strained or inimical, a reverse process takes place in which one group tries to do the opposite of what is practised by the other. This is called contra-acculturation. While acculturation characterised the relations between tribals and non-tribals in the earlier phase, contra-acculturation came to characterise their interactions in the recent years. The reasons are exploitation and mistrust. Until these causes are removed, amicable relations cannot be restored between tribals and non-tribals.

It is hoped that the material presented in this treatise will make the leaders of different sections of people to come together and put in their best efforts to build bridges of understanding between different ethnic groups in the State of Tripura and build a new Tripura State ensuring harmony and peace which are essential for development, This is the only way to ensure a meaningful future and happiness to the children of Tripura.

AGARTALA, TRIPURA
23 AUGUST 1990

K.V. RAGHUNATHA REDDY
GOVERNER OF TRIPURA

Preface

I ventured to write on the subject of tribal extremism in Tripura with special emphasis on the socio economic and political upheavels in the State. This attempt was made on the basis of experience I gained during my research career in the field.

I am fully conscious of the fact that the subject is controversial and sensitive. Yet, I have made an earnest effort to focus the pertinent facts and also to highlight the truth in the greater interest of the nation. Both the Central and the State Governments have now seriously undertaken various developmental projects and welfare measures for upbringing the tribal peoples. But for an effective planning for the implementation of the tribal welfare measures, a scientific study is indeed a desideratum. The present study shall serve as a background for the preparation of any plan for developmental and welfare projects. To begin with attempt has been made to introduce the State of Tripura with particular reference to its land and people including an account of its landscape, geological and geographical features. This is necessary for presenting a picture of the physical and cultural environments in which the tribes of Tripura have been living from remote antiquity. The ethnographic features including cultural characteristics of the tribes of Tripura have been presented in Chapter II. It is on this background that the traditional socio-economic profile of the tribal peoples with particular reference to their food gathering, food producing activities, handicrafts, textile-weaving, exchanges etc. has been portrayed in Chapter III. It is on this perspectives an account of the immigration of non-tribal population has been dealt with in chapter IV. While dealing with the immigration of the people, particular emphasis has been laid on social acculturation and impact or modernization in the behavioural pattern of tribal life. It has been attempted to explain as to how and why the rulers of the State of Tripura encouraged the Bengali Hindus to settle in Tripura. In this context while dealing with the transition in the tribal life from primitive agricultural life to modernity, the administrative aspects and also the inadequacies of safeguarding measures for the tribals have been reviewed. The analysis shows that the picture in respect of the safeguards is highly disappointing. It has been observed, that because of cultural advancements, the tribal peoples have become more conscious of their rights and privileges. Gradually, a new tribal national feeling of consciousness has grown in them and this has been kindled by some foreign agencies. This is followed by an account of tribal extremism since 1767 to the recent Mandai Massacre of June, 1980. This extremism has been presented in two distinct phases. The first phase lasted from 1767 to 1946 while the period from 1947 to 1980 formed the second phase. Reference has also been made on the formation of the Dinesh Singh Committee along with its recommendations to resolve the basic problems of the State. The great tribal uprisings of 1980 being accompanied by large-scale devastation and killing of hundreds of men and women by the TNV extremists and their political aspects have been treated in chapter-VII and chapter-VIII. It has been also shown as to how the Government of India during the tenure of Shri Rajiv Gandhi's Government brought about settlement of the tribal problems by the historic 'Peace accord' signed by Shri Bijoy Hrangkhawl and five other TNV leaders on behalf of the Tribal National Volunteers (TNV) and Shri P. Srivastav, Additional Secretary to the Government of India, Ministry of Home Affairs in presence of General K.V. Krishna Rao (Retd.), Governor of Tripura and Shri Sudhir Ranjan Majumder, Chief Minister of Tripura in New Delhi on 12th August, 1988. At present, the tribal extremists have no doubt cooled down but the anti-non-tribal feelings still persist among the tribal communities of Tripura. This has been considerably hampering the progress of the developmental works in the State. So, the immediate need of the time is to remove all tribal discontent, anger and hatred against the non-tribals and for this some positive suggestions have been made in the last chapter entitled 'Tasks Ahead' with special emphasis on the point that the basic policy should be to integrate the tribal people and to bring them on a par with all other sections of the great Indian nation.

I am profoundly grateful to Shri K.V. Raghunath Reddy, Governor of Tripura, who in spite of heavy engagements kindly provided me with a thought provoking and learned Foreword to this book. I acknowledge my sincere feelings of gratitude to my teacher, Shri S.K. Choudhury, retired Principal, M.B.B. College, who took great pains to read the manuscript and also for making many helpful suggestions.

I shall be failing in my duty, if I do not express my deep sense of gratitude to my teacher, Dr. J.B. Ganguly, Vice-Chancellor, Tripura University. He has always been a source of encouragement for me.

I wish to record my gratitude to Shri Banamali Sinha, P.O., A.D.C., Agartala, Sri Pulin Behari Debnath, Secretary, Governor's Secretariat, Tripura, Sri Rajkumar Panchamjit Sinha, Dy. Director, Information, Cultural Affairs and Tourism Department, Agartala, Dr. Pradip Bhattacharya, R.O., Tribal Welfare, Sri D.P. Deb Burman, L.O., Tribal Research Directorate, Agartala, Shri Sailesh Ch. Bhattacharya, Office of the C.S., Agartala, Shri Subir Choudhury, Head Librarian, Shri Motilal Chakraborty, Librarian Accountant Shri Chitta Ranjan Debnath, M.B.B. College, Agartala and Shri S.N. Sarkar, Gian Publishing House, New Delhi and many other friends and students who have helped me in various ways in writing this book. For any shortcomings in this work. I am, however, entirely responsible.

It will also be not good on my part, in case, I forget to express my thanks to my wife Smt. Jayanti Bhattacharya and my daughters Suman and Sona who always inspired me with love, faith and prayers. Finally, I must express my indebtedness to my parents whose inspiration and blessings have enabled me to complete the present work.

SUCHINTYA BHATTACHARYYA

Contents

ONE

LAND AND THE PEOPLE

The State of Tripura is situated in the North-eastern region of the subcontinent of India. It lies between the latitude of 22°56'N and 24°32'N and longitude of 91°10'E and 92°21'E. Northern, Western and Southern sides of Tripura are bounded by Bangladesh and on East by Assam, Mizoram and the Chittagong Hill Tracts of Bangladesh. The maximum length from North to South is 183.5 kms., and the maximum breadth from East to West is 112.7 kms. (Map 1). An international boundary line of 839 kms. separates the State from Bangladesh on North-West, West and South-East. The land surface linking Assam and Mizoram on North and North-east covers an area of 162 kms. The present territorial area of the State of Tripura is 10,477 sq.kms.[1]

Name and Origins

The origin of the name of Tripura cannot be ascertained with certainty. A mythical account of its ancient history is contained in the Rajmala or the Chronicles of the Kings. According to Rajmala it was King Tripur, the 39th descendant of Dhruya who gave the Kingdom the name that still bears. Modern Scholars, of course, doubt the authenticity of many of the accounts chronicled in this mythical story. They, for example, hold that the ancient rulers who are mentioned in the Rajmala as rulers over Tripura prior to the Muslim rule in Bengal, are all imaginary and fictitious. Hence, it is difficult to accept the King Tripur as a historical figure.

According to Lewin, the word *Tipperah* is pronounced and spelt in Bengali as *Tripoora.* The Sanskrit term *Tripoorardona* is used to denote the Sun, and as the worship of the Sun seems to have formed a part and parcel of the culture of the Hill Tipperah, it is not an improbable hypothesis to suppose that the name *Tipperah* might have been derived from *Tripoorardana,* the Sun God.[2] The common belief is that the name Tripura is derived from the Goddess *Tripura-sundari,* the presiding deity of the land. This appellation was given by the Aryan speaking immigrants or by the neighbouring Aryan settlers of the lower Bengal. But this view cannot be wholly accepted because the country had been known as Tripura even before the installation of this deity. It is more plausible that the deity in question was named after the country.

Sinha (1896), a chronicler of Tripura gives a different opinion altogether. According to him the term *Tripura* is derived from two Tipra words *Tui* and *Pra.* According to *Tipra* tribal community *Tui* means water and *Pra* means near, and thus, the term *Tripura* means a land adjacent to water.[3] It is said that in olden times, the boundaries of Tripura extended upto the Bay of Bengal when its rulers held sway from the Garo Hills to the Arakan Hills. So, it is not unlikely that the name of country was derived from the nearness of its territory to water, and its inhabitants came to be known as *Tipras* called after the country, i.e. Tripura. It is again believed that the name Tripura is a Sanskritised form of *Tipra,* a tribe to which the ruling family belonged.

Geological Perspectives

Geologically, Tripura is a part of the North-eastern India. Its Northern part is characterised by sedimentory rocks which are grouped into three : The *Surma* Group (further subdivided into the *Bhuban* and *Bokabil* formation), *Tipam* Group and *Dupi-Tila* Group. The above rocks range in age from Middle Miocene to Recent, i.e. from 18 million years to less than 1 million years old. The *Surma* Group consists of indurated sandstone with 50 per cent grey and olive clay rocks. The Tipam sandstone is associated with lumps of silicified fossil wood. It comprises medium yellow to light buff and brownish yellow rock. The *Dupi-Tila* Group consists of brown to buff sandy clay with greenish and reddish brown sandy loam followed by mottled sandy clay.[4]

The rock formation of the Southern District range in age from Mid Tertiary (15 million years) to Recent (1 million years old) age. The Southern District as a whole comprises ***argillaceous*** and *arenaceous* sedimentary rock like sand-stone, shale and clay belonging to the *Surma* Group, *Tipam* Group, and ***Dupi-tila*** Group. A major portion of this district is occupied by the Recent alluvial deposits. The sedimentory rocks are deformed and folded.[5]

Tripura's Western District is represented by sedimentary rocks range in age from (25 million years old) Miocene to loosely consolidated sediments of Recents (1 million years) age. The rocks are sandstone and siltstone shale grading into clay. These rock types are repeated as layers one above the other. It appears from the nature of grains and textures imprinted on these rocks that originally sediments were deposited in the sea and later converted into rocks which were subsequently acted upon by strong forces and resulted in the folding of the rocklayers into wave-like structures known as Anticlines and Synclines.[6]

Hills

It may be noted that before its merger into the Indian Union, the State was called *Parbatyo Tripura*. As implied by its name, the country is hilly. About 70 per cent of the area consists of hills and small hillocks, and the rest of the area is plain-land situated in the river valleys and the narrow strips of land between the tilas is known as *Lunga-land*. There is no proper mountain as such. Some peaks in the eastward ranges rise upto a height of more than two thousand feet. There are again series of hill ranges running parallel to one another from North to South dividing the State into broad valleys. The ranges increase in height towards the South from the plaines of Sylhet and towards the North from Chittagong District in Bangladesh. The hills are narrow ridges and sometimes so narrow at the top that it is very difficult to walk over.

The principal hill ranges from East are : *Jampui*, *Sakhan-Tlang*, *Longtarai* and *Atharomura* running through Hill Tripura in northerly direction and almost parallel to one another. The Northern portion of the valleys between the above ranges are mostly flat, swampy and covered with runk vegetation and in the South these are of a wild and broken character intersected by an infinity of deep-cut ravines and narrow-topped ridges. The highest peak is *Betling-Shiv* about 3,200 feet above the sea-level. It gradually decreases in height both ways. To the North it is joined by small *tilas* or hillocks with a low ridge which runs into Sylhet and to the South with the range of Chittagong in Bangladesh.

Land

About 70 per cent area of Tripura consists of hills and small hillocks, the latter being called as *tilas*, and the rest of the area is plain. On the basis of cropping pattern, the land of this area may be classified into three main categories : (1) *Tilla* land or small hillocks, (2) Plain land and (3) River Valleys. The *Tilla* land again can be further divided into two types (i) The *Jhum* cultivation (shifting cultivation) areas on hills and steep hillocks and (ii) Flat-tila i.e. table land. The *Jhum* cultivation is resorted to by the tribals who sow paddy seeds, sesamam, cotton, maize, chillies and other *Kharif* vegetables whereas in the flat *tilas*, the Kharif is the main crop. Plain-lands are divided into three classes : (i) high plain land, (ii) medium low land and (iii) *low-lunga* (plain land situated in the river valleys and narrow strips of land between the *tilas* is locally known as lunga).

Soil

The soil is mainly laterite in the hills and hillocks and alluvial in the flat land. In the valleys, soil is medium to fine in texture and light grey in colour and contains more organic matter than the *tila-soil*. The soil of the plains locally known as nal (arable) can be described as loamy with less sand-content than the *tila-soil*. The soil of the Lunga-land is generally acidic, and its texture is course to medium. It is important to note that about 98 per cent of the soil contents tested were found to be high about (0.75%) to medium (0.5% to 0.75%) in respect of organic carbon and medium (224.5 to 561.37kg) in respect of available nitrogen. More than 50 per cent of the soil are low (below 22.4 kg.) in available phosphorous and 80 per cent low (below 112.3 kg) in available potash.

Forests

Tripura, was once abounded in luxuriant forests. These were mostly naturally grown forests and yielded a very important addition to the State resources. But at present, due to repeated and indiscriminate *Jhum*-cultivation by the tribals and high demand for land for settling the refugees from Bangladesh, the forest produces, as such have decreased to a considerable extent. Now only a small quantity of soft wood is obtainable and exported to Assam, and the remaining forest produce is utilised locally. The Forest Department, however, has undertaken plantation of rubber, cashew nuts, coffee etc. which hold out the prospects of a lucrative cash crops.

As regards types of vegetation, the forests of the entire State may be classified into five major types : (i) East Himalayan Lower Bhabar-Sal, (ii) Cachar tropical ever green forest, (iii) Moist mixed deciduous forest, (iv) Low alluvial Savannah woodland, (v) Moist mixed deciduous forests-dry bamboo brokes.[8]

Rivers

The State of Tripura is bereft of any river of worth mentioning. There are only several rivulets, some of which may be called rivers by courtesy. These rivers are not again navigable by any boat of four tonnes capacity throughout the year. During the rains, the hilly rivers become full to the brim with tremendous current and tend to get flooded. In other seasons, most of them remain practically dry except in some sections. The principal rivers in the State are : (i) the Gumti ; (ii) the Haora ; (iii) the Khowai ; (iv) the Manu ; (v) the Feo ; (vi) the Longai ; (vii) the Juri ; (viii) the Muhuri an (ix) the Feni. It may be noted that none of these rivers of the State has undergone any great or sudden changes in its course and none of them forms any island and there is no regular inland water-traffic in the State nor any water-side town fed by any river.

The Climate and Rain Fall

Tripura falls within the tropical climate Zone. The climate moderate with high humidity. During the winter season temperature varies between 22.5°C (77.09°F) and 10.4°C (50.7°F).[9] From the month of March, temperature rises rapidly and reaches the highest point in the month of May. The period from March to May is the Summer season in Tripura. At the end of the summer, the South-West monsoon sets in and lasts upto September. The last monsoon season covers the months of October and November. During the months of April and May, humidity varies between 50 per cent to 75 per cent, but during monsoon it is over 85 per cent.[10] The rainy season commences from the beginning of April and continues till the middle of October. Practically speaking, the rainy season covers half of the year. The average annual rainfall in the State is 2100.7 mm (81.07"). But during the summer, the rainfall is generally accompanied by thunder storms. The highest temperature so far recorded at Agartala is 41.1°C which was on May 25, 1962 and the lowest is 5.2°C recorded on February 4 and 5, 1968.[11]

Flora and Fauna Bamboo

The State of Tripura with its characteristic physical features including its geological formation and dense jungle area is traditionally known as a great depository of various kinds of flora mostly grown in the forest areas of the various flora species. Two plant species viz., bamboo and cane are extremely important for two reasons ; firstly, these are widely grown throughout the State, and secondly, these are widely used for different purposes by all categories of people living in the State. Bamboo is widely grown in all parts of the State. Most of the hills produce different kinds of bamboos. It is interesting to note that the demand for bamboo is greater than any other botanical species available in the State. All kinds of people belonging to different social and economic positions are very much dependent on bamboo products. In the first place, bamboos are extensively used for building houses or huts or any kind of shelter by both the advanced and tribal peoples. Not only that, a peculiarity with the advanced people is that the boundary fencing is invariably done with the bamboo strips. Secondly, the traditional craft and industries of the Jhumias also centre round bamboo products.

In this context it is also important to note that the condition for germination, growth and development of rubber plantations are quite favourable and recently Tripura has earned a name in rubber plantation and already opened up a new horizon in economy. The tapping of rubber is very encouraging and the yield of later is even higher than the yield in Kerala, the home of rubber in India and not only that, the dry rubber content of Tripura latex is the highest in India.[12]

The fauna of Tripura bears a close resemblance to those in Assam and Bangladesh due to close continuity of the forest and ranges of the North-eastern border of the State with the Chittagong hill tracts and the hills of Southern Assam and plains of Western border of its territory with Bangladesh. There is hardly any peculiarity in respect of animal species of Tripura.

Tribal Communities

There are as many as nineteen tribal communities in Tripura. These are : Tripuri, Reang, Jamatia, Chakma, Halam, Noatia, Mog, Oraon, Santal, Khasia, Bhil, Bhutia, Lepcha, Chaimal, Lushai, Uchai, Kuki, Garo and Munda. According to 1981 Census Report of India, the population figure of the Scheduled Tribes was 5,83,920 i.e. 21.54 per cent of the total population. The following table will show the composition of the tribal communities since 1961.[13]

From the figures in the table it is evident that the Tripuris formed the highest percentage among the Scheduled Tribes followed by Reang, Jamatia, Chakma, Halam, Natia and Mog. The other tribes constituted very small per cent of the total population.

Tripuris who constituted the highest percentage amongst the Scheduled Tribes spread over in all the sub-divisions and their highest concentration was in Sadar and lowest in Dharmanagar. Reang, Noatia, Mog and Garo are to be found in almost all the sub-divisions. The highest percentage of Reangs and Noatia lives in Dharmanagar and Amarpur respectively. Kukis and Garos are mostly in Udaipur and Kamalpur sub-divisions. The concentration of Jamatia is maximum in Udaipur while Chakmas are mainly in Dharmanagar and Amarpur sub-divisions respectively. The tribes like Oraon,

Saptal, Munda, Khasia are chiefly in Northern District. The Mogs are chiefly confined to two sub-divisions viz., Sabroom and Belonia in the South Tripura District. The Halams are confined to Udaipur, Amarpur and Kamalpur, and Lushais are generally found in Jampui Hills in Dharmanagar sub-division. (Map 2).

Sl. No.	Name of Tribe	POPULATION 1961 census	1971 census	1981 census
1	2.	3	4	5
1.	Bhil	63	169	234
2.	Bhutia	7	3	5
3.	Chaimal	50	—	—
4.	Chakma	22,386	28,665	39,005
5.	Garo	5,484	5,559	7,124
6.	Halam	16,298	19,076	25,692
7.	Jamatia	24,359	34,192	45,487
8.	Khasia	349	491	642
9.	Kuki	5,531	7,766	9,985
10.	Lepcha	7	177	234
11.	Lushai	2,988	3,672	4,671
12.	Mog	10,524	13,273	16,934
13.	Munda, Kaur	4,409	5,347	7,124
14.	Noatia	16,010	10,297	12,963
15.	Oraon	2,875	3,428	4,671
16.	Reang	56,597	64,722	85,836
17.	Santal	1,562	2,222	2,336
18.	Tripuri	1,89,799	2,50,388	3,19,692
19.	Uchai	766	1,061	1,285
	(Unspecified)	—	36	—
Total :		3,60 070	4,50,544	5,83,920

Thus, the above analysis of the land, its physiography and people demonstrates that the State of Tripura is indeed the most fascinating region from both physiological and ethnological points of view. The physiographical conditions relating more particularly to hills and forests and also the fluctuating tropical climate with considerable rain fall provide a formidable resort to a post of hill peoples like the Tripuras, Jamatias, Reangs, Halams, Kukis with diverse physical features and cultural attainments. All these people though of foreign extractions had from indeterminable time made Tripura their primary habitat and from bygone days they have most wonderfully succeeded in retaining their respective indentities pertaining to their cultural traditions and physiognomy.

REFERENCES

1. Bhattacharya, A.K. : *Tripura, a Portrait of Population* (Census of India 1971), p. 185.
2. Lewin, T.H. : *The Hilltracts of Chittagong and the Dwellers Therein*, Calcutta, 1869.
3. Sinha, K.C. : *Rajmala*, Comilla, 1896.
4. Geological Survey of India: *Miscllaneous. Publication No. 30, Part IV*, Calcutta.
5. Geological Survey of India : *125th Anniversary Celebration Publication*, Agartala, 1976.
6. *Ibid*
7. Chakraborty, R.N. : *First Working Plan for Udaipur Forest Division*, Agartala, 1971, p. 3.
8. *Ibid.*, p. 22.
9. Menon, K.D. : *Tripura District Gazetteers*, 1975, p. 757.
10. *Ibid.*
11. *Ibid.*
12. *Draft Annual Tribal Sub-Plan*...1987-88, Government of Tripura, p. 1
13. *Ibid* , p. 1 to 2.

TWO

ETHNOGRAPHIC FEATURES OF THE TRIBES

Though the determination of physical characteristics, ethnic affiliations and culture of the tribes of Tripura is not the primary concern of the present dissertation and yet a brief study on it is essential for a proper appraisal of the tribal communities of the State. There cannot be any doubt about considerable admixture and cultural intermingling of tribes but the individuality of each tribe is well demonstrated if one happens to make a scientific analysis of any one of these peoples. In the following pages, a brief discussion is made on the ethnographic features of some of the important tribes of Tripura.

The Tripuris

The Tripuris are numerically more predominant than the other Scheduled tribes of Tripura. In 1981 Census Reports, the number of the Tripuris has been recorded as 3,19,692. Ethnologically the Tripuris are affiliated to the Bodo tribes of Tibeto-Burman group who spread over the whole of the Brahmaputra Valley and North Bengal, forming a solid bloc in North-eastern India.[1] The Anthropologists are of the opinion that the Bodos appear first to have settled over the entire Brahmaputra Valley and extended West into Koch Bihar, Rangpur and Dinajpur Districts of North Bengal.[2] Again from Nowgong District in Assam, their area of occupation extended to Cachar District and into Sylhet and from Cachar and Sylhet they extended further to the South to Tripura State where there is still a Bodo speaking in the shape of the Tripura tribe which founded the State and from Tripura they spread into Comilla and possibly also Noakhali Districts of Bangladesh and thus they occupied the mouths of the Ganges of the Eastern sea.[3]

The Tripuris are divided into two groups viz. *Puran* Tripuris and *Natun* Tripuris. The former rulers of the State emerged from the *Puran* Tripuri community. The *Natun* Tripuris came into existence at later periods as a result of admixture between the Tripuris and the Bangalees. The Tripuries are sub-divided into twelve *Haddas* or groups according to their vocation related to the throne viz., Bachhal, Siuk, Koatia, Daityasing, Hazuria Silatia, Apiya, Chhatratulya, Deoral or Galim, Subenarayan, Sena and Jalal. It is important to note that the above classification of the Haddas are disappearing due to the loss of the princely State.

Ethnically, the Tripuris are characterised by Mongoloid features like scanty hair on face and body, flat face with prominent cheek bones, arrested development of nasal bone and epicanthic fold. Regarding stature, it has been found that the majority people of this community belong to short statured group.

The Tripuri dialect commonly known as *Mrung* belong to Tibeto-Burman group,[4] comprising Tibetan-Himalayan, Assam-Burmese and North Assam Branches. But, though akin to the above branches, the Tripuri dialect contains variations in intonation and accent. The differentiation, however, might have been caused by the physiography of their land, habitat and ideals. As a matter of fact, dancing and singing cover the whole range of their life from birth to death-remarkable as well as most trivial events in life.

As regards religious beliefs and practices mention may be made that Tripura has been an arena for the expression of some of the highest qualities of the Indo-Mongoloid people under Hindu inspiration. According to Dr. Chatterjee (1950), "the Tipras like the other Bodo Groups had their tribal religion much modified by Hinduism. But among them and under the aegis of the ruling house of Tripura a good deal of their old pre-Hindu religion and its rituals is preserved as part of the State Religion".[5] The 'national pantheon' of the Tipras consists of a group of fourteen gods who are worshipped by the *Chantai* or high priest in a series of fourteen metal heads in a temple at old Agartala form the Tipra Palladium.[6] It is important to note that the use of the heads only, in lieu of full images is something unique in Hindu ritual, and this thing is also found elsewhere in Tripura e.g., heads carved on rock at Unakoti near Kailasahar of North Tripura District and in South Bengal in the cult of Dakshina Raya, the God of Tigers-probably an *Austric* cult in origin.

The Reangs

The Reangs are next to Tripuris from the point of view of numerical importance. In the Census of 1981, they numbered 85, 836.

The traditions of the Reangs represent them as a race wandering from one land to another until they found their present shelter in Tripura. They are mainly concentrated in the sub-divisions of Kailasahar, Amarpur, Belonia, Khowai, Kamalpur, Udaipur, Dharmanagar and Sadar.

The Reangs belong to the Mongoloid racial stock. They are migrants from Burma and entered into the State of Tripura most probably through the Chittagong Hills. According to Deb Burman (1931), "the Reangs after migration from Chittagong Hill Tracts settled first in Amarpur sub-division in large numbers and prior to that used to live in Mayanithlong of Lushai Hills".[8]

On linguistic grounds the Reangs have been classed with Tibeto-Burman group and the dialect is known as *Polong-O*.[9] They are divided into two major groups viz., *Meska* or *Mechka* and *Marchhai* or *Malchhui*. The first group is again sub-divided into seven groups e.g. (i) Tuimaiyafak, (ii) Mechka, (iii) Mesa or Muchha, (iv) Raichak or Rai Kachak, (v) Takh Mayakcha, (vi) Waring or Wariem and (vii) Charki. The Marchhai group is also divided into seven sub-groups viz., (i) Murchhai, (ii) Apet, (iii) Nakhya or Nagkham, (iv) Chamrong, (v) Darbong, (vi) Sagrai and (vii) Reang or Rai Kachak. It may be noted that the co-tribes or sub-tribes of the Reangs are so much in common both in language, manners, customs and system of internal Government, that it is absolutely necessary to take them together.

In the Reang community the above fourteen *dafas* or groups have their own chiefs who are known as *Rai*. Each dafa looks to the *Rai* as its own monarch whose word is supreme in all matters. The other lower ranks of the *dafa* are : Chapiakhan, Chapia, and Darkalim. Succession is not hereditory and it is determined by the qualities of leadership. Thus, within their own social fold, the Reangs are a very disciplined community and as a result, they are least affected by feuds and dissensions.

The Reangs generally select hills or hillocks locally known as 'Tila' for their habitation. The idea behind such selection is based on the question of security, water supply and ready availability of food. In the past, every village was exposed to constant danger of being taken by surprise by new bands of people in search of settlement in a new place. Naturally, they would select such places which have natural protection. So hilly tracts covered with dense forest were normally preferred for the location of their villages. This selection was again influenced by the prime necessity of life i.e. water. Therefore, the locations which were considered most suitable were hill tops with a gentle slope leading to a river or *chhera* (rivulet) and jungles on the background. The typical hut which is built on a high bamboo platform is commonly known as *Tong-ghar*. The measurement of the *Tong-ghar* varies 40'×18' to 8'×4' in length and breadth respectively depending upon the number of families living in it. The ground plan is rectangular and the materials used in their construction are bamboos for piles and walls of the hut. The gabled roof on the otherhand is thatched with *Sangrass*.

The Reang boys marry at about the age of twenty-twenty one. Girls are given in marriage at an early age. A girl is considered to be marriageable when she can carry water with two earthen pitchers together. The types of marriage which prevail in the Reang community are : *Chamraikomi* (marriage by service), *Hamjook tooba* (marriage by the payment of bride price); *Chamari tooba* (marriage by the payment of bridegroom price), *Hamjok teisao* (marriage by abduction), *Teikhalaio* (love marriage), *Tei Kharo* (marriage by elopement), *Boorai Selaioi laga* (marriage by mild capture), Sindoor foolna (remarriage of widow). Although there are eight modes of marriage but system of marriage by service (Chamrai komi) is most common. According to this system, the bridegroom has to serve in his father-in-law's house for the period of three years as a suitor. During this period he tries heartily to please all the members of the girl's family. He takes special care to please his mother-in-law because much is dependent on her opinion and if the boy is found fit and partners like each other, the marriage is solemnised. In case, the boy is unsuitable, he is sent away from the bride's house and whatever might have happened is simply forgotten.

Like the Tripuris the principal occupation of the Reangs is *Jhum* cultivation. Generally, during November-December each household selects hill slope for jhum cultivation. The selected hill slope is known as *Oakha*. After site selection, they worship *Burachhu*, the presiding deity of jhum for rich harvest. Preparation of the field is followed by sowing on an auspicious day. *Jhuming* is a multi crop cultivation such as Khul (Cotton), *Mai* (Paddy), Chalkumarh (Gourd), Khakolu (Pumkin) etc. Both the sex work together in the field. They do not feel boredom. They celebrate two festivals which are directly related to their cultivation. One is held prior to the commencement of the Jhum and the other is held after the new crop has been harvested which is similar to the *Navanna* (new crop) festival of the Bengalees. Again, once in a year the Reangs assemble at one place to celebrate the worship of *Tripurasundari* or *Lakshmi* or *Ker* or the goddess of river. Although, this is a religious congregation but in actual practice this is nothing but a social get-together where the whole community feasts, sings, dances and drinks to the last and exhausts whatever might have been kept away as provision against a rainy day.

During the princely rule, the Reangs constituted one of the strongest pillars of the State's military forces and they were much respected for their marital qualities. Here mention may be made of two Reang Generals of Maharaja Dhanyamanikya (1463-1515) viz., *Raikachak* and Raikachham who were well known in the history of Tripura. These two Generals defeated the invading army of Hussain Shah, the Sultan of Bengal in the 15th Century.[9] The Reangs are also widely known for their loyalty to their chief whose word is supreme in all matters of internal disputes. It is important to note that in the administration of the Reang Community, there is no place for hereditory rulers. On the other-hand leadership is determined by the qualities of a leader and as such they are the choice of the people by democratic process.

The Jamatias

Ethnologically, the Jamatias are akin to the Tripuri or Tipra tribe. The term *Jamayet* is an Arabic word. It means assemblage or mobilisation. It is believed that a section of the Tripuris was considered very brave and loyal and as such they were recruited in a large number in the State's military force which was called *Jamat* and subsequently they came to be known as Jamatiyas. Anthropologists are of the opinion that the influence of Arabic became prominent in this region only during the rule of the Nawabs of Bengal. The continuous fighting between the Kings of Tripura and the Muslim rulers of Bengal paved the way gradually for this Arabic language to penetrate to Tripura and thus casting its influence to a great extent.[10] Of course, some leading personalities of the Jamatia community are of the opinion that when Pub Narayan, the legendary figure of the Jamatiya community brought the image of *Biyagwang Goriya* (one of the popular deities of the Jamatiyas) from the land of Kukis by exhibiting great valour and presented it to the King, the king ordered him to worship the deity in a *Jamayet* i.e., in a assemblage form and since then those persons who were worshipping the image of Goriya in a group came to be known as Jamatiyas.[11] Hence, there are controversies, no doubt, regarding the origin of the term *Jamatia* but the fact remains that during the princely rule the army personnels were given a special position amongst the tribals and were also exempted from *Ghar-Chukti* (House tax) and given settlement mainly in Udaipur, the capital town of Tripura. As a result of this the members of the State's military force who mainly belonged to the Tripuri tribe managed to evolve a political system of their own and developed economically and socially.[12] There is also historical evidence that when Udaipur was the capital of Tripura, army personnels were given permanent residence round the capital. At that time the system of monthly salary was also not in vogue, instead, such persons were given land settlement around the capital. This assemblage of the community gradually established matrimonial alliance and blood relationship among themselves and ultimately developed into a separte endogamous community.

The Jamatia society is patrilineal and patrilocal. The family is nuclear in character and monogamy is the rule, though polygamy is not unknown. A Jamatia woman shares with her husband the socio-economic activities of the family. The exclusion of Jamatia woman from certain religious festivals and ritualistic observances like their periodical segregation during their periods appears not to be due to any assumed inferiority in their status but due to the tribal's horror of menstrual blood which is supposed to attract evil spirits.

The main occupation of the Jamatias is *Jhum* cultivation. Hunting and fishing are important only as diversions. Their agricultural technique is the same as that of the Tripuris. Their chief crop is rice. Fish form important article in diet. Various kinds of traps are in use for this purpose. Dried fish is considered a special treat.

The Jamatias have been profoundly influenced by Hindu culture. They accepted Vaishnavism during the reign of Maharaja Bir Chandra Manikya (1861-1896). Historical evidence, shows that the Jamatias rose in revolt against the autocratic rule of Maharaja Bir Chandra Manikya under the leadership of Parikshit Jamatia.[13] The Maharaja, however, succeeded in crushing the rebellion. Since then the whole community accepted Vaishnavism. In this context it is also important to note that their traditional ritual activities are officiated by the *Achai* (tribal priest) while non-traditional rituals are performed by Brahmin Priest Thus, they are facing the transformation with the least possible disturbancss.

The Chakmas

The Chakmas, the fourth largest tribal group in Tripura numbered 39,005 according to 1985 Census. Anthropologists are of the opinion that they are Arakanese-immigrants and were either pushed westwards or were forced to seek new domains along the western littorals. This is evidenced by their largely inhabitance in the central parts of hill tract of Chittagong which is contiguous to the Hills of Arakan or Arakan Yoma in Burma.[14] Of course, according to their traditional belief their original home was in the southern hill tracts of Chittagong along the Matamuri river and then gradually they came in large numbers to Tripura in search of *Jhum* land where they form an important section of the people. In the State of of Tripura, they are concentrated mostly in Kailashahar, Amarpur, Sabroom and Dharmanagar. The whole community is sub-divided into eight groups viz., Malima, Tauja, Barua, Koda, Wuangsa, Buma, Kurchya and Kadua. The above groups, however, have no major difference in respect of manners and customs.

Like all other tribes of Tripura the Chakmas are also dependent on agriculture, being the synthesis of early are cultivation i.e., shifting cultivation and settled cultivation. At present, the Chakmas, however, in large number are opting for agriculture through plough cultivation on a permanent basis.

Within their own social fold the Chakmas are a very disciplined community and this explains why the Chakma community suffers so little from internal feuds and dissensions. They have their own form of internal Government based on a system of well defined hierarchy. The head of the community enjoys the title, *Dewan* and weilds enormous powers. The Chakmas look up to him as their own monarch whose word is supreme in all matters of communal disputes, petty thefts and minor offences. The next officials in the line of succession are : *Khijayas*, *Talukdars*, *Karbaris* respectively.

Adult marriage is prevalent among the Chakmas but child marriage is also allowed by them though the custom is not very common. Marriage life is generally settled by the guardians and the conjugal life of the Chakmas is peaceful and harmonious.

The Chakma women are experts in weaving and use their own hand-woven clothes while the malefolk have taken to mill made dresses. Ornaments used by the women are similar to those of the Bengalees. Their food habits is somewhat comparable to those of the Kukis but they are not addicted to drink as the Kukis. They mainly depend upon jhum for livelihood. Hunting, fishing and minor cottage industries such as basket making, etc., are the most important subsidiary occupations.

The Chakmas cremate deadbody and in case of necessity, the body is placed in a wooden box for several days with the purpose of enabling the relatives to be present in the funeral rites. The social custom being that the members of the family of the deceased offer gifts according to means.

Most of the Chakmas are Buddhists excepting a very few who profess either Hinduism or Christianity. The supreme God is Lord Buddha. It is important to note that although the Chakmas are Buddhists by religion, yet they have developed a fine synthesis of Hindu, Buddha, Vaishnavism and even Islam in their religious performances.

The Halams

Numerically, the Halams occupy the fifth place in the list of Tripura tribes. According to the Census Report of 1981, the total number of Halams is 25,692 (projected figures) distributed over different parts of the State.

The Halams are mostly affiliated to the Kuki group of tribes of north-eastern India, but on their settlement in Tripura they have changed considerably. Philologically the Halam language is of Tibeto-Burmese origin. It is generally admitted that the Kukis who acknowledged the suzerainty of the Kings of Tripura came to be called as Halams. But, now the term *Halm* is commonly applied to denote only the subjugated tribes of Tripura. There are controversies amongst scholars regarding the derivation of the term Halam. Some scholars are of the opinion that the word Halam is to be derived from the Urdu word *Salam* i.e. salutation. The Kukis who became loyal to the King of Tripura were called *Halam* because they used to bow down to the Tipra chieftain as an indication of their avowed submission and loyalty. Again, others think that the term *Halam* is derived from the Tipra words (Kak-Barak) *Ha* and *lam* ; *Ha* means land or earth's surface and *lam*, path. Hence, the word Halam denotes path or land. This derivative meaning of the term *Halam* may be interpreted as : The Kukis who were mainly food gatherers and hunters and accepted land as the only means of livelihood after their defeat at the hands of the Tipras and as such they were given the appellation Halam. Another derivative meaning of Halam may be found in the exposition that the submissive Kukis under the aegis of their new master were prone to protect such land (Halam) as their means of subsistence. This contention supports the observation of Chatterjee (1950) who upholds that the Kukis as the subjects of the Tripura Kings took a leading part in the struggle against the Mohammedans from Bengal, and the Kacharis and Jaintias from the north and the Arakanese from the south.[15]

It may also be noted that the ruling house of Tripura in recognition of the services of the loyal Kukis (Halams) used to hold a great community dinner every year on the night of *Vijaya-Dashami*. This community dinner is called *Hasam-Bhujan*. *Hasam* is a Tipra word denoting 'a soldier' and *Bhujan* means banquet held in honour of the soldiers. It is on this occasion that the people belonging to all tribal groups used to be invited. But a privileged position in this feast was accorded to the Halams in commemoration of their submission and loyalty to the Kings of Tripura and their war-like spirits. It appears that Halams in the past constituted the strongest base of Tripura's army and the King also for maintaining a close personal relationship with his army personnels might have held their dinner on the aforesaid auspicious day. But since independence, this ceremony has been discontinued.[16] In this context it is also important to note that at present, a good number of Halams use even the surname Singha to elevate their position as *Kshatriya* or army personnel. It is very interesting to refer that by an order (No. 34) of the 10th Awsina 1336 T.E. (1946 A.D), the King of Tripura, accepted the assumption of *Singha* surname for all the members of the Halam community.[17] But some Halams still prefer to call themselves Kukis to which group they originally belonged. They are, however, called, *Mila-Kukis* i.e., the mixed Kukis.

The Halam dialect is cogante to the Kuki language of the Naga group. Though akin to the Kuki language, the dialect contains variations in intonation and accent. These differentiations might have been caused by the physiography of their land and habits. However, according to Grierson's classification of the languages of the hill tribes, the Halam dialect falls in the Assam-Burmese group of Tibeto-Chinese family.[18]

The homestead of the Halams consists of a group of dwellings without a common yard. They have a nomadic attitude towards home. From the very beginning the Halams were in the habit of changing village sites. A new village site is indicated by a new house. A household has one or more dwelling huts, each of which faces east or north in accordance with the traditional customs of the communities. In some houses specially of *Tong-ghar* there is no separate room for cooking or store or guest room but definite areas are set apart for the specific purpose of cooking or storing. No part of the house is reserved for the use of women or children. Of course, the house has partitions from pile to pile with the purpose of reserving accommodation for head of the family, elders, youngers, sons, daughters, new couples, guests, etc.

By the tradition, Halams are forest dwellers. Hills and forests have shaped the habitats and economy of the tribe. Most of the activities pertaining to food quest are performed in the hills and forests. Fruits, leaves, roots and tubers which supplement and balance otherwise their predominantly cereal diet are obtained from the forest. The wild animals which are the food items of Kaipeng dish are found in the dense hilly forest. Again fish, a delicacy in Halam diet are caught in small streams or *chheras* and waterlogs. Mostly, hills and forest supply the prime necessity-namely food to the Halam community.

The Halams believe in the existence of soul after death and that belief becomes clear from a study of their funeral rites and practices. Both the practices of burial and cremation are found prevalent amongst the Halams. The sections of the Halamas which is closely affiliated to the Kuki tribe, generally practices burial for the disposal of their dead. But the Halams in general follow the practice of cremation. Those who practices burial believe in the existence of a land supposed to be a replica of their world, a little away from grave yard of the dead whose soul is again supposed to take refugee in that land. Accordingly, all possessions including even wartrophies, food articles and drink, utensils etc. of the dead are offered to the soul.

The Mogs

The Mogs mainly inhabit in the southern sub-divisions of Tripura. They are said to have descended from the Arakanis who in turn trace their origin from the same line of *Kshatriyas* in which was born Lord Buddha. The Burmese chronicle of *Maharajoang* and the Arakan chronicle of *Rajoang* lend support to this popular story. According to Anthropological observations, the Mogs are, however, the offshoots of Tailongs who were driven out of China towards the south and south-west.[13] The earliest home of which they have any definite traditions is Arakan, whence they migrated early in the Seventeenth Century into Cox's Bazar of Bangladesh. There they again split up. Some migrated further into British Bengal, while two other sections entered the Chittagong hill tracts. The first to arrive were the Southern Mogs under the leadership of the chief of the Phru family of the Ragretsa clan. They occupied the Chittagong Hill District while the Northern Mogs moved north and north-east and finally settled in Southern Tripura which is adjacent to Chittagong hill tracts of Bangladesh.

According to 1981 census the Mogs numbered 16,934 (projected). They have a language of their own belonging to Burmese group of Assam-Burmese branch of Tibeto-Chinese family.[20]

The Mogs are by nature hardworking, very simple, generous and hospitable. The headmen are generally known as *Bomang Chowdhury* or *Tahasildar*. They are elected on the basis of their wealth and social distinctions. The headmen are supposed to maintain internal discipline and look after the welfare of the community. Women enjoy a great deal of freedom. They are strong, stout and industrious. In addition to their household duties they help their husbands in agricultural activities. In leisure time they weave their own garments.

The pattern of a Mog village is a scattered one. The reason for such pattern may be attributed to the fact that Mog village surroundings are covered with dense forests and naturally, the villagers are bound to take extra precaution for preserving their agricultural products and with this object in view the households are scattered around their paddy fields. They live in a group of 5 to 70 families and the area of settlement is known as *Pohochu.* It has been observed that all huts excepting *Keyang* (Place of worship) are for residential purpose. Huts are constructed both on mud plinth and on piles. In every household there are two or more dwelling huts, a kitchen shed and a haystack. The dwelling huts are generally east-facing according to the traditional custom. It is interesting to note that in some Mog villages dormitory still exists. The dormitory is locally known as *Sabosa-ing* and every dormitory has its leader who is popularly known as *Sabosa-gong.* Any youngman who is physically tough, good natured, intelligent and mentally strong is selected a *Sabosa-gong* by the elderly members. Among the girls, there is a separate association which is led by *Aseragong* only. Asera means leader. Of course, girls are not allowed to stay in *Sabosa-ing.* They remain with their respective guardians at night.

The traditional clothings for a Mog women are *mamarngi* or *bakkabrabangi* and *roomal. Mamarangi* is used for covering the upper part of the body and whereas the *roomal* which is like a *Pachra* of the Tripuri Community is used to cover the lower part of the body. The malefolk on the other hand puts *lungi* on the lower part and stiched garment on the upper part. They are also found to cover their head with unstiched cloth in the form of a *turban.* Unlike other tribes they are famous for their showy and colourful dresses. Both males and females have special fascination for dazzling garments. Another interesting feature is that they practise tatooing. Men are tatooed on their arms and women on the back of their shoulders and on their hands. These refer to some speciality or achievement in their society.

Like the other tribes of Tripura e.g., the Tripuris, the Noatias, the Mogs are also patrilineal and patrilocal. They are in general monogamous in character, though polygamy has a social sanction. Cross cousin marriage in prevalent and a man can marry his father's sisters daughter but he cannot marry his mother's brother's daughter who is also a cross cousin. Parallel cousin marriage of any form such as father's brother's daughter or mother's sister's daughter is totally absent.

The Mogs are Buddhists by religion and their ritual performances are done by Buddha Bikshu. The supreme God whom they worship is *Phora* (Buddha). While other important deities are *Sani* or *Chini*, *Kali* and Ganga (Mheong). In every sphere and activities of life, the worship of *Phora* is indispensable. In almost every village there is one Buddha temple characterised by a single-roomed hut thatched over with a four-sloped roof made of tin or *Sangrass* designed in the form of *Pagoda*. According to the traditional rule, a confirmed bachelor is selected as the priest of their temple. He is known as *Shamphura*. The priest is however, assisted by one or two assistants in the management of the temple. The significant point lies in the fact that the *Shamphura* and his assistants not only practise asceticism in quest of salvation but they are also solely responsible in imparting traditional education to the children of the community. Such education includes social norms, manners, discipline and finally the essence of solidarity.

The Lushai

The Lushais were originally inhabitant of the Mizo Hills district lying to the east and north-east of Tripura. In primitive times they were known as Kirats. The name *Kirat* was given by the plain-settlers of Bengal. The people of Cachar call them *Luchais*. *Lu* means head and *chai* means to cut. Hence, the word Luchai means a head hunter. The word *Lushai* is presumed to have derived from *Luchai*. There is historical evidence that even as late as the middle of the nineteenth Century, the Lushais used to hunt heads at the time of funeral of the chieftains.[21]

The Lushais are said to have come from Mizo hills to Tripura due to availability of plenty of fresh *Jhum* land. The traditional belief among the Mizon (Lushai tribe) is that they originally came from *Chhing-lung* meaning 'covering rock' which may perhaps be a place now called Silung in China bordering Shan State in the east. Before they came to the present land, they lived in the hill tracts of Burma bordering the present Mizo district between the Run and the Tiau rivers.[22]

The traditional occupation of the Lushai community is jhum cultivation. Of course, some Lushais have already taken to plough cultivation in addition to jhuming and hunting. They generally live on the hillocks in a group of five to fifty families. The houses are built about 2 to 3 feet above the ground and have wooden planks. Now-a-days some people are settling on the plains and erecting houses like the plains people, adopting their methods of cultivation.

The Lushais practise monogamy but till recently they insisted on keeping more than one woman. The first woman whom one marries is considered by the Lushai society as his wife and the children born out of this union are called *Chhung-puit*. Any woman living with a man for cohabitation without being married to him is considered his concubine and the children born out of their union are called *hmeifa*. Usually after marriage, a son lives with his parents till some dispute arises or a brother junior to him gets married. This type of family is known as stem family which stands at intermediate stage between elementary family and joint family.

The Lushais are a patrilineal people. The Lushai family consists of members related to each other by blood, marriages and adoption, all having the same social, economic and religious status under a single head. A male member is under the direct authority and control of his agnatic kin, his father, father's brothers and other male members of his own lineage. As the property passes from father to son and as father pays bride-price for his son, son always tries to abide by the wishes of his father.

The staple food is rice with some green leafy vegetables or some millets, etc. They are very fond of meat. Beef is a delicacy reserved for big feasts and ceremonies only. The Lushais do not like cow milk. *Zu*, the locally made rice beer is very favourite to them. The local cigarettes and pipes are very common in the villages. The Lushais are also very musical minded people and sing their songs very sweetly to the accompaniment of guitars and Ukuleles. In education, the Lushais have gone far ahead of the Kukis and as a result of the spread of education their general level of culture and accomplishment has much improved. Christianity has spread fast among the Lushais and they have taken to Western dress and manners.

The Kukis

Next to the Lushais the most important groups of tribes are Kukis. The term Kuki, according to Shakespeare is not accepted by the people concerned. They rather call themselves *Hre-em.*[23] They are known as Kukis to the Bengalees and other plain living people. The Cacharis call them *Lushais.* The Manipuris call them *Khongjais.* In the Chin Hills and generally on the Burma border they are called China. The Kukis are also known as *Darlongs* in Tripura and the Tripuris call them *Sikam.* As a matter of fact the term Kuki is more particularly used to denote the various tribal peoples who were successively driven out from the Lushai and Chin Hills into the sorrounding regions in the direction of north and west. The tribes first dispersing from the Lushai land into Cachar, the Ranghols and Betes with their shots are generally called old Kukis and the term new Kukis became affiliated to the Thados, Jangshena and other tribes migrating subsequently.[24] Sopitt (1893) contend that the appellation Kuki was given only to a few traders who came across as Lushai. But the general plains people never saw them and as such, could not ascertain their name from those few traders. It is quite but natural that these people changed their name to suit their convenience. As a result of transformation, the Lushai first became Lakai then Kukai and finally Kuki.[25] Hence, it is agreed that the words *Lushai* and *Kuki* do not actually signify two different tribes ; they mean the same group of people with a common racial stock.

The Kukis as a tribe are in fact divided into fifteen clans[26] e.g. (i) Paitu, (ii) Belathat, (iii) Thangulus, (iv) Lalifang, (v) Bangkhai, (vi) Mizel, (vii) Namtu, (viii) Chatya, (ix) Phun, (x) Kunteri, (xi) Lentai, (xii) Jangtei (xiii) Rangchan,

(xiv) Balte and (xv) Khoreng. It may be noted that out of groups, people belonging only to the first five clans are found in Tripura. And as a process of more simplification they may further be divided into two broad categories : Lushais and Darlong Kukis. This is evident from the observations of Grierson (1927) : "It seems at least very probable that Khelama and Sakajaib are nothing else but Halams".[27] In this connection, it would be very interesting to refer to the observation of the Political Agent of Tripura (1873) who specially stated in his official correspondence that the Halams in Tripura were undoubtedly of Kuki origin. Their language is a mere dialect of the Kuki and a Kuki and a Halam can readily understand each other. Thus, the above contention lends support to the identity of the *Halams*, of Tripura with the Kukis.

The Kukis are generally found today in Dharmanager, Kailashahar and Amarpur sub-divisions. In 1981 census the Kukis were enumerated as 9985 (projected). They are expert archers and also adept in using spears. Their main occupation is jhum cultivation and hunting. Usually, they live on the top of the hills in house built on a bamboo platform 5' to 6' high above the ground. Another important feature is that they do not repair their houses but when they become unfit for habitation they just build new houses on a new site only.

he bond of unity among the Kukis is very praiseworthy. The *Sangalthongs* or the village leaders settle all kinds of disputes within the village. There is also a village council under the leadership of *Sangalthong* in every village. Inter village disputes are settled by the *Ujirs* who are appointed by the Kuki *Raja* or *Lal* for a certain area but during the reign of Tripura *Rajas*, separate Raja or Lal of the Kukis was appointed by them. He would control and look after the Kuki customs and interests and for his all activities he is responsible only to the Raja of Tripura who seldom interfered with the internal autonomy enjoyed by the chieftains except that the latter were required to pay nominal homage to the State ruler once or twice in a year as token dependence. Not only that, the courts of the ruler also had no effective jurisdiction over them who would on the other hand, settle their disputes and social squabbles internally under the direction of the local chieftains. In this context it may also be noted that during the princely rule, the *jhumia* of Tripura did not pay any revenue for land. Instead they paid house-tax or *Ghar-chukti Kar* annually to the Rajas of Tripura but the Kukis were even exempted from the payment of house-taxes on the ground that they used to render military service when required. In support of this contention reference may be made to the observation of Dr.Chatterjee (1950) : "The Kukis of Tripura as subjects of the Tripura Kings took a prominent part in the fight the latter gave to the Mohammadans from Bengal and to the Kacharis Jaintias in the North and the Arakanese in the South.[29]

The Kukis are accustomed to putting on very few clothes. Women ordinarily cover the waist and the knees with small pieces of cloth, while the rest of the body is laid bare. Malefolk remain almost half-naked. The ornaments used by them are carved out of tusk of elephants and boars. There is also a custom among them to make a hole in the lobe of the ear and bigger holes in the ear, is considered to be more beautiful than others with small ones.

They had a curious system of burying their dead bodies particularly when a chief was to be buried. Generally, the deadbody of the chief was placed in a huge dug-out log and encircling the log, a ring of fire was made and the fire was kept burning for three months. After such a ritual the bones and skin of the deceased were buried in a pre-selected hole with tribal pomp and barbaric grandeur when cut-off heads of the plain dwellers were thrown into it. There is a historic evidence that in 1844, the Manipuri village of Kochabari was raided primarily for this purpose by Lal Chokla when his father died. The matter was, however, ended when British troops entered Tripura, captured Lal Chokla and transported him for life.[30] At present, however, such a custom is no longer in vogue.

The Garos

Anthropologists believe that the Garos originally belonged to the Garo Hills. The word *Garo* is said to have derived from Garo one of their original leaders.[31] Of course, according to traditional Garo belief, the first man to settle in the *Garo* habitat was Bona Nirepa Jane Nitepa (Rongmuthu 1960), also the first man to start shifting cultivation in which he was aided by the deity *Misipa.*

The Garo dialect belongs to the Assam-Burmese family and is placed together with *Bodo* groups. At present the Garos are mostly found in Sadar, Kamalpur, Kailashahar, Udaipur and Amarpur.

They live in houses built on high level ground with clearly defined boundary. The dwelling houses are made of plaited bamboo-splits with two thatched hempen roofs. The main occupation of the Garos is agriculture. Shifting cultivation still prevails in the remote areas. There are archaeological evidences to show that in very early times shifting cultivation was practised in Garo habitat. In support of this statement the observation of Majumdar (1976) may be made : "Neolithic celts of various sizes and shapes have been found all over the Garo habitat and this stone implement is very much like the iron hoe used by the Garos of the present day".[31] Hence, there is no doubt that the present day Garos were shifting cultivators.

As regards, religion and culture the Garos are divided into four sections viz., (i) Sonsanrik, (ii) Baptist, (iii) Catholic and (iv) Hindu. Very recently, a good number of them have embraced Christianity. The Hindu Garos worship Hindu Gods and Goddesses. It may, however, be noted that like the other tribes of N.E. India, the traditional Garo religion was also nothing but a way to obtain crops and to keep away diseases and disasters. Hence all operations of shifting cultivation were performed with religious awe and the series of annual rites and festivals were linked with different religious rites in the plot. As for example the *Agalmaka* rites were performed in connection with the burning and planting of jhuming. Again, the *Miamua* rites are performed by the *nokma* i.e. the representative of the land owning class at the time of harvesting. Thus, it is evident that the traditional Garo culture was in complete harmony with shifting cultivation.

The above resume cf the ethnographic features of the tribes of Tripura clearly indicates that these though of foreign extractions had from indeterminable time made Tripura their prrmary habitat. A scientific study of even one of these tribal communities would reveal an apparent diversity in cultural assemblages, but a key note of fundamental unity in respect of physiognomy and general cultural behavioural patterns prevails among all these tribal communities of Tripura.

REFERENCES

1. Chatterjee, S.K. : *Journal of the Royal Asictic Scciety of Bengal*, Vol. XVI, 1950 No. 2, p. 172.
2. *Ibid.*
3. *Ibid.*
4. Grierson, G.A. : *The Linguistic Survey of India*, Vol. III, Part III Delhi, 1927 (1967), pp. 1-2.
5. Chatterjee, S.K. *J.P.A.S.B.* Vol. XVI, 1950, No. 2, p. 218.
6. *Ibid*, p. 219.
7. Bhattacharya, A.K. *Tripura: A Portrait of Population Census of India*, 1971, p. 159.
8. Thakur, S. Deb Burman : *Bibarani* (1340 T.E), Agartala, p. 71.
9. *Ibid*, p. 148.
10. Bhattacharya, P.N. : *The Jamatias of Tripura*, Directorate of Research, Tripura, 1982, p. 4
11. *Ibid.*
12. *Ibid.*
13. Thakur, S. Deb Burman : *Census Biborani* (1340 T.E), Agartala.
14. *Ibid.*
15. Chatterjee, S.K. : *J R.A.S.B.* Vol. XVI, Calcutta, 1950, No. 2, pp. 221-222.
16. Sen, K.P. *Rajmala*, Vol. II p. 47.
17. Menon, K.D.: *Tripura District Gazetteers*, Agartala, 1975 p. 175.
18. Grierson, G.A. : *The Linguistic Survey of India*, 1927, pp. 330-331.
19. Mills, J.P. : Notes on a tour in the Chittagong Hill Tract (1926) *Census Report of India 1931*, Vol. V part I pp. 515-517.
20. Grierson, G.A.: *The Linguistic Survey of India*, Vol. III part. III.
21. Menon, K.D. : *Tripura District Gazetteers*, Agartala, 1975.
22. Roy Burman, B.K. : *Demographic and Socio-economic Profiles of the Hill areas of North-east India*, New Delhi, 1970, p. 84.
23. S.B.K. Dev Varman : *Directorate*, Tripura, p. 20.
24. Grierson, G.A.: *The Linguistic Survey of India*, Vol. III part III p. 1-2.

25. Soppitt, C.A. : *A short account of the Kuki-Lushai Tribes on the North-east Frontier 1893* (Reprint 1976), p. 1.
26. *Ibid.*
27. Grierson, G.A.: *The Linguistic Survey of India*, pp. 1-2.
28. Hunter, W.W. : *A Statistical Account of Bengal*, London, 1876, (Reprint 1973), pp. 488-489.
29. Chatterjee, S.K. : *J.R.A.S.B.*, Vol. XVI, 1950, p. 222.
30. Menon, K.D. : *Tripura District Gazetteers*, Agartala, 1975 p. 157
31. Majumdar, D.N. : *Shifting Cultivation : Is it a way of life ?* An analysis of Garo Bata, North-East India Council for Social Science Research Shillong, 1976, p. 12.

THREE

THE TRADITIONAL SOCIO-ECONOMIC PROFILE

The tribals are, by tradition, forest dwellers. The surroundings in which they live have conditioned their life-patterns in such a way that they have not yet been able to come-out of the fetters of primitive economy which primarily consists of food-gathering, food producing, animal domestication, cottage industry, etc. As a natural process, the food-gathering activities of the tribals is supplemented by the primitive methods of agriculture known as shifting cultivation or *Jhum* cultivation. A perusal of their economic pattern also reveals that they are economically self-contained and self-sufficient. They make their own articles of daily use without any help from available extraneous sources. This naturally implies that they make or produce their own requirements of non-agricultural goods in their cottage industries. Today, however, it is very difficult to live in an economic isolation and the tribals also are not an exception to that. Money economy has considerably changed the nature and character of the economic life-patterns of the Jhumias who also have become prone to outside cultural influences. This would be evident from the survey of the economic activities of the tribes of Tripura under such headings as food-gathering, food production, handicrafts, textile-weaving, exchange and tradings.

Food Gathering Activities

Food-gathering activities of the tribals mainly consist of collection of fruits, roots, tubers, leaves etc. from the nearby hillocks or jungles, hunting animals and birds in the hills and forests and fishing in the neighbouring rivulets.

Food Collection

It may be noted that the collection of fruits, roots, tubers or leaves etc. is mainly done by womenfolk of the society, but in case roots lie too deep in the soil, they may take the help of malefolk. Of course, it is not uncommon that sometimes the adult males and boys extend their help and cooperation in food-gathering activities of the women.

Strenuous activities like plucking fruits from trees or collecting honey from hives are done by men and boys only. It is significant to note that the food-gathering patterns of the Jhumias of Tripura are mostly common to all other tribes of North-east India like the Sema, Nagas, Angami Nagas, Kuki Lushai, Lakhers, Purums and analogous food gathering activities are also to be found amongst Lamets of South-east Asia.

Collection of Honey

The collection of honey by the tribals is also very interesting. This is done in the months of June and July. When a bee-hive is detected on a tree, several men mostly young-boys go to remove it. One who is expert in climbing, climbs up the tree and drives away the bees with the help of a burning torch made of dry bamboo and leaves. Others on the ground also help in driving out the bees by burning torches and when the hive is completely free from the bees, the climber removes the hive by a bamboo silver or a *takle* (iron chopper) and places the pieces in a container which is mostly a loin cloth. The hive is then distributed equally among the members of the hony gathering party.

Wild Products including Medicinal Plants

Other wild products which are collected by the tribals are : *Raichuk* (soft top of cane), *Samasata* (ceatella asiatica), *Thalik Balang* (wild banana, *Musa Rosea*), *Ganga* (wild root), *Muitu* (arum), *Muia* (bamboo sapling), *Banskurul* (bamboo shoots) etc. It is important to note that the roots and tubers are collected during the Winter season, when there is a scarcity of food-grains. Besides these roots and tubers the Jhumias collect some medical plants which are mostly known as folk-medicine. Amongst them worth mentioning are : *Abroma augusta, Aegle marmeloes, Bacopa monneleria, Terminalia arjuna, Mucuna Prorita T. Chebula, Zingiber officinales, Piper niagrunm, Ipomia aquatica, Oxalis Corhieulata*[1] etc. It is interesting to note that even today, the tribals do not bother for the treatment of any disease. They have a great belief and reliance on their folk medicine.

Hunting

The next important food-gathering activity is hunting of birds and animals. Almost all animals excepting certain species like tiger, monkey, crow etc., are hunted for food. Of course, the tribals do not always hunt birds or animals for food-gathering purpose but for protecting the Jhum crops against them. It is important to note in this context that a certain section of the Jhumias, viz., the Kaipengs do not usually kill a tiger. They consider that they themselves are the descendants of tiger.[2] If, they hear that a tiger is killed, they observe mourning for a period of three days and do not pertake anything other than *nera-mishi-chanai* (vegetarian food) during this period. They also cry aloud for the killed tiger. It is thus evident that doubtlessly the Kaipengs had tiger as their totem, and as such they consider themselves as its descendants. That is why a distinct taboo on killing or eating the tiger persists among them even today.

As a matter of fact, hunting activity is closely associated with the life-pattern of the tribals of Tripura. The tribals start practising it from childhood. The elders teach and impart training to the youngsters regarding the use of weapons and traps during the hunting operation. The youngsters never miss an opportunity of joining any hunting expedition. The tribals hunt both individually and collectively. Women and girls are not, however, permitted to participate in any hunting operation. Only the adults and the grown up boys engage themselves in hunting expedition. Generally, small games like deer, boars, hare etc. are hunted by an individual. In the case of hunting any big animal, they organise themselves into a huntig party. To ensure success, they perform some magical rites with the purpose of pleasing the *Lagri* deity (Goddess of fortune). The tribals strongly believe that if *Lagri* is pleased, they will have nothing to fear and they would be able to entrap or kill wild animals very easily.

Fishing

Another important activity is fishing which prevails so widely among all sections of the tribal people that it may well be taken for all practical purpose as a primitive method of gathering food. This is not restricted to only among the males as in hunting, but unlike hunting, fishing, operation is open to both sexes. Both males and females go out in groups for fishing throughout the year, especially during the rainy season when the rivers overflow and marshy areas become filled with water. The presence of *lungas* (marshy places) and *chheras* (streams) in and around the village encourages the Jhumias to pursue fishing activities and very often they postpone Jhuming in favour of fishing. Sometimes, almost all the villagers engage themselves in fishing. This is mostly of a communal fishing i.e. fishing operation being conducted by the whole community. In such a communal fishing operation, the gains are equally divided amongst the participants.

Food Production

Although the tribal people are mainly concerned with the food-gathering activities and their economy centres round it, yet they are not averse to the primitive type of producing food articles by Jhum cultivation, yields of which are not again sufficient enough for their subsistence. Naturally the tribals, known as Jhumias are mostly dependent on food gathering which is supplemented by jhum yielding crops. It is important to note that the tribals produce food crops by an incipient type of agriculture on the slopes of hills and jungles, which is a very common primitive practice of food production in North-eastern India, South-east Asia and also in some other parts of India and outside. This kind of food production is called by the primitive peoples of north-eastern India and also of Tripura by the name *Jhum* which means shifting cultivation, i.e. the area under cultivation is shifted from one selected field to another, the primary reason being the loss of fertility after at least two seasons of productions.

For a proper understanding of the *Jhum* cultivation, it is necessary to give a brief account of the different stages of *Jhum*-production as pursued by the Jhumias of Tripura. This may be noted as follows : (i) Selection of *Jhum*-field and its associated rituals ; (ii) Tools used in *Jhuming* operation ; (iii) preparation of the field ; (iv) Digging of holes and sowing of seeds ; (v) sprouting and weeding ; (vi) provision for protection of *Jhum*-field ; (vii) Crop-harvesting and (viii) Threshing and storing.

Selection

It is important to note that while making the selection of a *Jhum*-field, the Jhumias always take into account such factors like a virgin site bearing bamboos and bushes on the hill slopes and secondly, the selected *Jhum*-field must be in the vicinity of the dwelling place for the purpose of keeping constant watch over the field and making all sorts of provision for the protection of the crops. Of course, the liberty of selecting *Jhum*-field has been presently very much restricted by the Forest Department which actually allots plots of lands to the individual Jhumia families for Jhum cultivation.

The selection of the Jhum-land is completed by the Jhumias during the months of November and December. But the final selection of the land for *Jhum*-operation is, however, closely associated with some magico-religious beliefs and practices. The Jhumias believe in the existence of the Goddess of the *Jhum*-field. So, before undertaking any operation, the Jhum deity, also known as *Bura-Devta* is worshipped at the very site which has been preliminarily selected for *Jhum*-cultivation. It is a very simple kind of worship. First of all, a small area of the selected field is cleared and made clean. Then, three short bamboo pieces are planted in the ground. Generally, the bamboo pieces are planted in horizontal row at a distance of 12 inches from one another. These bamboo pieces are supposed to represent the Goddess of the *Jhum* field. In the next stage, the owner of the *Jhum*-field, keeps in his hand splitted two halves of a bamboo piece. He then drops down two halves of the bamboo pieces with the chanting spells.

Now, if one half of the bamboo split falls on the ground obversely or reversely, the site would be considered unsuitable. This practice of throwing bamboo pieces is to be continued thrice, and if the auspicious signs as indicated above are not obtained, the site is abandoned and a new selection of another field is made. It may be noted that this type of ritual practice is also common to many other tribes of North-eastern India.

Tools

As regards tools and implements it may be mentioned here that previously the only tools used for Jhum-cultivation were : the digging stick and a chopper. By the digging stick, holes are dug out in the Jhum-field for sowing seeds, and the chopper is used primarily for cutting plants, bushes etc. But, now-a-days, the Jhumias rarely use any digging stick, and even the chopper used by them is made of iron which is locally called *Takal.* Othe iron tools used in *Jhum*-cultivation consist of *Cekhras* (Sickles). Besides, these cutting and digging tools, baskets made of bamboos and canes are also used for carrying and holding seeds to be sown.

Preparation

For the preparation of Jhum-field the Jhumias, first of all, clear the field by cutting down all plant and bushes which are left in the field to be sun-dried for several days (not less than twenty-five days to thirty days). This practice, however, requires to be followed only in the case of a new Jhum-field to be cultivated. For sowing seeds a second time in the same field, there is hardly any need for any clearance on such a wide scale. Whatever, may be the case, when it is found that plants and shrubs are fully dried, fire is set for burning for four to five days and two to three days are required for cooling down. Burnt ashes are considered to be good manure for the fertilization of the soil which would promote bumper production. After cooling down, the burnt ashes are then evenly distributed over the entire field of operation and levelled up. This operation is to be completed by the month of Falguna i.e. February-March.

Digging and Sowing

The next stage is meant for digging and sowing. It is only after the first rains that preparations are to be made for sowing seeds and the day for sowing is to be fixed in accordance with the Omens or dreams of the head of the family. If he dreams clear water, fish, paddy or or cooked rice then it is considered auspicious for sowing operations and the *Jhum*-field thus prepared is also considered to be a potential one. On the other hand, if the head of the family dreams an animal killed by a tiger or a broken *Takal* or a dying domestic animal, pigs or fowls being stolen etc., these are considered inauspicious indications for the same and accordingly, another day is fixed for sowing operation. The Jhumias pursue two methods of sowing seeds viz., (i) broadcasting, and (ii) sowing in dug-outs. As regards the first method, it may be stated that seeds are held in a bamboo-basket called *Japa* by the left hand, and seeds are taken out of it by the right hand and broadcasted by walking up and down the entire *Jhum*-field. After this broadcasting of seeds, the Jhumias would expect a few showers which would help in covering seeds thus sown with soil and also in sprouting. If there be no rainfall tendershoots would wither away and thus sprouting and growth of plants by broadcasting seeds is sohely dependent on rainfalls.

The second method relates to the digging of holes in horizontal rows, up and down the field and placing seeds inside these holes and finally covering holes by the dug-out loose earth. Previously, these holes used to be dug-out by the *latha* or digging stick but now-a-days, *Takal* or iron chopper is commonly used for digging holes in the Jhum-field. These holes are dug in rows at an approximate depth of 3" at a distance of 18 inches from one another in horizontal rows beginning from the top of the field and ending at its bottom. A still more common practice with the Jhumias today is to dig holes with the *dao* or a kind of iron chopper which is an all purpose cutting tool used so commonly by the plains people. The usual practice is that holes are dug and seeds are placed inside the dug-outs which are thence covered with the dugout loose earth. While sowing seeds, the basket commonly known

Japa, containing the same is held on the left waist, and the digging and sowing are done by the right hand. It is to be borne in mind that for the participation in this sowing operation, there is no taboo on women and as such, both men and women are to be found merrily engaged in sowing operation in the *Jhum*-field.

Sprouting and Weeding

It has been found from common experience that germination or sprouting requires at least fifteen days or so from the date of sowing. Thick sprouting and weeds growing are not at all congenial or rather harmful to the healthy growth of plants. Accordingly weeding is a must for the healthy growth of plants which can alone yield bumper crops. Weeding is primarily done with hand, i.e. weeds and undesirable sprouts are simply uprooted and the base of each plant is cleared for its full growth. Very often the iron chopper or *Takal* is used for the purpose of weeding. Among the Jhumias, weeding is a primary concern of the women and children who are engaged in this operation often for the whole day at a stretch. This weeding operation is continued thrice at an interval of one month or so, normally in the months of June, July and August. But the number of operations to be undertaken depends largely on the growth of any other plants. After the completion of the weeding operations, plants are allowed to grow and bear fruits.

Jhum Protection

When plants start bearing fruits, there is the necessity of affording all sorts of protection to the *Jhum*-fields against the onrush of animals and birds. When fruits become mature, the *Jhum*-field falls prey to all animals and birds. Accordingly, the Jhumias adopt all sorts of protective or defensive measures in respect of their *Jhum*-fields. The most important protective measures undertaken by the Jhumias is to keep a constant watch over the *Jhum*-fields and to drive-out all animals and birds approaching the fields. For this, they build a watch-house either in the centre or at one side or at the corner of the *Jhum*-field. Such a watch-house is also called *Dandi*, measuring about 2' × 6'. It has a do-chala type of thatched roof and a platform without any fencing walls. For bamboo poles are planted vertically at a height of 10 feet and four such poles are tied horizontally to these vertical posts and then again bamboo poles are placed cross-wise upon this horizontally tied up bamboo poles to form platform. Upon this platform is raised the thatched roof. For climbing up the high watch-house, the Jhumias use bamboo poles placed in a slanting position from one side of the house to the ground. The watch-man stays in watch-house and keeps watch over the *Jhum*-field. It is interesting to note that the watchman drives out birds and animals from the *Jhum*-field by making all sorts of sounds like loud cries, hand clapping etc. Sometimes, watch-dogs are set-out for the same and fire is also set to drive them out. Besides, another method is adopted for making a peculiar sound for driving out birds and animals. For this, bamboo poles with the upper portion of each splitted into four parts are vertically planted in the field and a long rope is tied to all these splitted parts. When the watch-man pulls the rope, a peculiar sound is produced by the clapping of the bamboo poles. Frightening sounds thus produced drive away birds and animals from the *Jhum*-fields.

Traps are also commonly used for catching animals approaching the *Jhum*-field. One popular trap for this purpose is *Mankhang* which is set near a fence. A long and heavy log is placed in a slanting position, one end of which rests on the ground, and the other end is placed horizontally on another bar acting as a balancing rod. A board of bamboo poles and splits are placed below the log and heavy log and the balance rod serves as the connecting media between the log and the tread-board, the board presses the horizontal bar which releases the log causing its fall, and as a result, the animal becomes entrapped.

All these are a few means and methods by which the Jhumias protect their *Jhum*-field against animals and birds It goes without saying that the methods of protecting *Jhum*-fields described above are not peculiar to the Jhumias of Tripura, but the other Jhumias like Lushais, Kukis, Lakhers, Purms of North-eastern India also pursue analogous techniques for protecting their *Jhum*-fields.

Harvesting

The Jhumias produce varieties of vegetables and paddy including sesamum, nuts, cotton, etc. Sowing of seeds, growth of aforesaid plants and their yielding of fruits are all primarily seasonal. Accordingly, jhuming activities continue for a long period, and the harvesting operation also extends over different months of the year, more particularly from June to October. Traditionally, a Jhumia harvester used to carry a long conisal shaped basket called *Langa* on his back kept hanging by fastening it with a string of fibre around the head. The usual practice was simply to break ears and put them in the *Langa.* Now-a-days, of course, the Jhumias have acquired the use of iron sickle called *Cekhra* from the plains people and with the aid of the sickle, the Jhumias now cut each plant at its base. Fruits from the yields are subsequently seperated from ears by threshing.

Jhum-harvesting is a communal affair and generally all members of the family aided by the other villagers of the community participate in harvesting operations. It has been already stated that Jhum-harvesting covers a period from June to October and various yields are harvested in different months. As for instance, *Thaichumu* (cucumis), *Mamphal* (melon), *Sasha* (cucumber), *Magdam* (maize) etc. are harvested during the month of June only but *Maisinga* (sugar cane), *Khakloo* (white gourd), *Chalkumra* (pumpkin) etc. are harvested in the month of July. Again, *Mai* (paddy), *Chiping* (sesamum), *Despia* (hibiscus), *Mesta* (jute), *Khool* (cotton) etc., are harvested during the period from August to October.

Threshing

Harvested yields are brought home and kept in heaps for threshing. The threshing operation is restricted primarily to the members of the family concerned. The Jhumias pursue different methods of threshing. The simplest method is called 'treading', i.e. treading over ears for separating or detaching crops from the plants. Ears are spreadover the open courtyard and both men and women continue treading over them till corns are separated from ears. Another method is known as 'beating', i.e. corns are separated from ears by beating with a wooden or bamboo rod. Both these methods are very primitive practices which are followed even today by the Jhumias of different parts of the North-east India.

Winnowing

When separation of corns from ears is over, the Jhumias keep themselves busy in winnowing operation. The traditional method of winnowing grains is by sprinkling them in the air in the direction of wind blowing. This would result in falling down of solid grains on the ground separately because chaffs and other unwanted light contents are blown away by wind. Besides this natural method of winnowing, an artificial practice has been also taken recourse to. This relates to the use of a winnowing fan which is even now a common practice amongst all rural peoples. These two methods of cleaning grains from chaffs may thus be described as winnowing and fanning. After clearing away all unwanted contents, grains are spread over the courtyard either on the ground itself or on a mat for drying in the sun. This is essential for the purpose of storing grains in a granary, called *mai-nok*. Generally, it is built at a corner of the courtyard and at a little distance from the place of cooking so that it may not catch fire.

HANDICRAFTS

It is evident from the discussion of the food-gathering and food-producing activities that the tribal economy is self-sufficient and self-contained and this is again revealed in other spheres of economic pursuits like general handicrafts and making of tools and weapons which are essential requisites for their very existence. In the field of handicrafts as well, the tribals do not make anything in excess of their needs. They generally make an article only to replace the old or unusuable one. Further, because of the self-contained economic pattern prevailing amongst the tribals each and every member of a family is also acquainted and well-skilled in all sorts of craft-making which are essentially required by them. In other-words, the tribals do not purchase any tools or any other essential articles from any extraneous agencies.

Food Gathering Tools

As regards traditional tools, first of all, we may, mention the tools and other accessories made and used by the tribal people for their food-gathering pursuits. The most important tool used by them for gathering roots and herbs from the jungle is of course, the digging stick (*Khura Latha*). A digging stick is made out of a particular species of solid bamboo bearing uniform girth. This bamboo species is called *Barak* (*Bambers block Roxb*). For making a digging stick, a straight and matured bamboo is to be selected. Generally the length of a digging stick ranges from 50 cm to 60 cm with a diameter of about 7 cm., the lower end of which is made sharply pointedin order to make the digging operation more effective. With the help of this digging stick the Jhumias dig all kinds of roots, herbs, etc. from the jungles for their consumption. Again, to carry home all gathering made in the forest, the Jhumias use a type of a carrier or a sort of basket, with the aid of which the Jhumias carry all sorts of articles. This kind of basket is roughly oval at its opening or mouth and it gradually narrows down to the base which is flat and circular. This kind of basket is made of thin bamboo splits and the technique employed is a simple twilling. The basket is carried in a hanging position from the shoulder under the arm-pit and held by a strap. It is no doubt an all purpose carrier basket.

Hunting Tools

Tools weapons used by the tribal people are indeed very few and simple. Only two kinds of tools are made and used by them for hunting purpose : (i) Bow and arrow and (ii) Spear. The bow is made from a single piece of a bamboo sliver. Its stave is about one and a half meter in length and the middle portion is oval in cross-section. The arrow shaft is made of the same kind of a bamboo as the bowstave. The shaft itself is rounded and polished. Sometimes, the arrow-head is poisoned by a compound made from a fluid derived from putrefacted heads of the snake, centipode, bee or wasp or any other dead animal kept in an earthen pot. The arrow-head is smeared with this poisonous fluid, and it is believed that such a poisoned arrow is most effective even in killing a large animal. The Jhumias are very expert in shooting arrows with the help of their bows and this is their only effective weapon for killing birds and animals. Besides the bow and arrow, the Jhumias are also accustomed to using spear which consists three parts : head, shaft and butt. The head of a spear has again three constituent parts like socket for the insertion of the shaft, shank and blade. The total length of each of these parts are : head-45 cm, blade-25 cm and shank-8 cm. The socket itself is about 12 cm. in length and the maximum breadth of the head is 9 cm. i.e. at the meeting of the shank with the blade. The shaft is again one and a quarter metre in length being rounded in cross-section with a diameter of 7 cm. This implement is made from a particular species of bamboo called *Muli* (*Melocanna bambusoides trin*) which is solid and maintains uniformity in girth.

Food Producing Tools

As regards tools for food-producing activities, it may be stated that the traditional tools required for food-production are also simple and very few in number. The primary tools required for food production activity consist of the cutting tool, digging stick, basket or *khara* and a kind of winnowing fan. These simple tools are sufficient enough for successful Jhuming operation for which there is hardly any need for any other complicated contrivances when the crops in the field ripen harvesting operation starts. Generally, the Jhumias tear the ears containing grains. Sometimes, *Chapraga* is used for separating grains from ears of the plants. This particular tool is made of a branch of a tree with three smaller branches diverging from one place. These smaller branches are brought to the same line and their upper parts are slightly curved by pressure. The user catches hold of the tool at the lower end and strikes paddy ears spread out on a mat or on courtyard itself. Besides, harvesting and threshing contrivances, the Jhumias are also accustomed to the use of husking-lever or *dhenki* which is very commonly used in the plains for husking grains. They are also in the habit of using mortar and pestle for husking but now they prefer dhenki. It is important to note that the tribal people are also expert craftsmen and as such they make their own tools and articles to be used for food-gathering, food-producing and household purposes.

WEAVING

The art of weaving amongst the tribals is absolutely a family concern and naturally so, the textile requirements of the members of each family are to be woven by the members of the family only. It is important to note that the art of weaving amongst them is a primary concern of the womenfolk. In fact, there is a taboo on man's participation. But in regard to the cultivation of cotton, carding of cotton flowers, spinning, yarning, dyeing, etc., men always help the women. Again, the making of the loom out of bamboo and wooden pieces is, however, the avocation of men only. Some believe that if men are engaged in weaving, the entire village may be visited by natural calamities or that the members of the family may suffer from all kinds of adversaries including failures in hunting operations or men may be killed by animals. Of course, a pragmatic explanation may be that men are always engaged in out-door activities, and as such, they have little time to devote themselves completely to weaving which is a long-drawn and time-consuming process. On the otherhand, the womenfolk are primarily concerned with the domestic works and accordingly, they can afford to have sufficient time at their disposal to engage themselves in all sorts of operations relating to weaving. That is why each and every family has a loom of its own for textile weaving.

Cotton Flowers and Cleaning

The raw material used for textile weaving is, of course, cotton. Every family procures cotton flowers from its plantation in the *Jhum*-field. Cotton seeds are generally sown in the month Vaishakha (April-May), and its flowers are plucked in the month of Paush (December-January). Then follows the collection of cotton flowers which are then spread over the ground in the court-yard for drying in the sun and these flowers are kept for three or four days in the courtyard for the same. When flowers are fully dried in the sun, operation begins for separating seeds from flowers. The next stage is to clean cotton flowers in a wooden gin with two rollers geared to revolve in opposite directions. Cotton flowers pass through the roller and seeds being unable to pass through it are left behind. After the separation of seeds, cotton flowers are teased with a bamboo bow to make them soft and fluffy.

Spinning Wheel

After cleaning, a quantity of cotton is rolled down in a cylindrical stick of about 12 cm. long and 1.5 to 2 cm. in diameter. These rolls of cotton flowers are then spun on a spinning wheel which consists of three parts, viz. base, wheel itself and spindle. The base of the wheel is generally made of two wooden pieces being rectangular in cross-section and dove-tailed at right angles near about the end of two other wooden pieces, heavier but shorter in length. At one end of the base two vertical wooden posts are inserted at one of the heavier pieces which are connected towards the top by a loose-fitted horizontal wooden bar being circular in cross-section. Both ends of this horizontal bar protrudes beyond the vertical posts, one of them being larger than the other. To this end the crank for moving the wheel is attached and the wheel rotates on the horizontal bar. The wheel and the spindle which is made of an iron bar, being circular in cross-section and pointed with one of its end, are linked up by a cord passed around it. The wheel is moved with the help of the crank which is held by the right hand. Thread is tied to the pointed end of the spindle and alongwith its movement the operator touches lightly the free end of the thread with one end of the sausage of cotton held by the left hand. At once the reed catches the loose fibres of the sausage and the left hand moves upwards and as a result, the yarning is done, which is then would round the spindle and the process is continued till the spindle is fully loaded with yarn. Afterwards, yarn is removed to a very simple tool made of bamboo or wood. This is followed by the next stage to dyeing. Colours generally used are : red, chocolate brown, black, dark-blue and green, etc. All these colours are produced from locally available floral and soft stone specimens.

Loom Operation

It is only after dyeing work, the womenfolk engage themselves in weaving clothes by a kind of loom locally called *Ri-thanthi.* This is a tension loom having the following parts : (i) two bamboo poles of 5' in height ; (ii) two horizontal bamboo beams about 3' or 4' long ; (iii) breast-rod which rests across the weaver's knees ; (iv) a back-strap or a belt made of hide which is tied at each end of the breast-rod and passed behind the back of the weavers ; (v) a rounded bamboo-split to which yarns are rolled ; (vi) a shuttle which is a short bamboo pipe into which the spool of yarn is placed ; (vii) neddle of bamboo ; (viii) a flat wooden plank with pointed ends measuring 30"×3' and (ix) lease-rod. The weaver sitting behind the breast-rod fastens each end of the two horizontal bamboo beams to a plaited cane-band. Then the loom operations starts. It may be noted that the breadth of a piece of cloth made from such a loom varies from 18" to 30" and its length is about 5' or 6'. Various colours are, however, introduced into the warp by laying out threads of different colours, but the woof is mostly of a single colour, either white or black. It has been already stated that the tribal people weave their clothings for their own consumption and not for any commercial purposes. Accordingly, each family meets the demands of its members in respect of clothings from the productions made by its own womenfolk.

BARTER AND TRADING

It has been already stated that the tribal economy is self-sufficient and self-contained and each tribal family is an economic unit with its own *Jhum*-productions, arts and crafts. It is interesting to note that previously tribal families were characterised by more communal in nature and character. When they were absolutely dependent on food-gathering and incipient food-producing economy, communal activities and endeavours in all matters relating to their means of subsistence were the usual norm. But it is only in the subsequent period that the individual tribal family unit emerged resulting in the transformation of the communal economy to family economy. Such an individual family economy was also self-contained and self-sufficient. It is again important to note that this individual family economic unit was not completely divorced from the larger communal economy. In respect of both communal and individual family economy, there had been little scope for any regular trading or exchange. In the case of primary needs, a tribal family would necessarily seek help or assistance in all matters either from other individual Jhumia-families or from the community and such a help or assistance used to be always given and was being extended even today. In fact, the communal character of the tribal economy is manifested in all aspects of their life and activities.

In course of time, again, economic developments have taken place to an extent of exchanging articles to meet the family needs. In otherwords, a sort of barter system developed amongst the tribal Jhumias. If a family was in need of a particular item, he could exchange another item at his disposal for the same. This barter system has been in practice amongst the tribals for a long time past. This is, of course, a very incipient kind of trading or exchange of articles by barter and this practice is being continued even today. It has been noticed the wandering hawkers from the plains move about from door to door in the tribal villages, more particularly during the harvesting seasons. The tribal Jhumias are also in the practice of purchasing articles from those hawkers by barter, i.e., giving them in return their own *Jhum*-produce. It may be stated that this kind of barter was a common practice amongst all the tribal families of Tripura and also the neighbouring regions of North-east India.

REFERENCES

1. Chakraborty, N.K. : Plant resources of Tripura Forests. (Article submitted in the Seminar on Planning for Forestry Development in the North-Eastern Region, Agartala, 1984) p. 3
2. Bhattacharya, S. : *The Kaipengs* (Published by the Directorate of Research, Agartala, 1980) p. 46.

FOUR

IMMIGRATION AND SOCIAL ACCULTURATION

In the preceding chapters, an attempt was made to present an analytical picture of the tribal life patterns in Tripura with particular emphasis on their identity, habitats, settlements, ethnic affinities, social organisations, and socio-economic pursuits. Besides, an attempt has been also made in this chapter to project the profiles of marked acculturation in the tribal life-patterns brought about by the immigration of population, especially, Bengali Hindus from erstwhile East-Pakistan, now Bangladesh.

Immigration of the People

It will be evident from the fact that according to 1981 Census Report the total population of Tripura is 20,53,058 and out of this, the number of tribal people has been enumerated as 5,83,920 i.e. 28.44 percent of the total population. A comparative study of the population figures as enumerated in the Census Reports from 1931 to 1981 shows a progressive decline in ratio of tribal population and rapid increase of the non-tribals and the ratio of the tribal population to the total population had never been static. This would be evident from the following table 4.1.[12]

It is significant to note that the non-tribal population of Tripura increased by 71.05 per cent during the period from

TABLE 4.1

Variations in Tribal Population Ratio

Year of census	Total population	Tribal population	Percentage
1931	3,82,450	1,92,249	50.26
1941	5,13,010	2,56,991	50.09
1951	6,45,707	2,37,953	36.09
1961	11,42,005	3,60,070	31.52
1971	15,56,342	4,50,544	28.95
1981	20,53,058	5,83,920	28.45

1961 to 1971; whereas India records a growth rate of only 24.5 per cent during the same period. On the other hand, the ratio of tribal population to total population of the State gradually decreased from 50.26 per cent in 1931 to 28.45 per cent in 1981 in spite of upward growth of population. This decrease in the population ratio in respect of tribal and non-tribal people of this State has been primarily caused by influx of people from the neighbouring regions of Bengal. After the partition of the country in 1947, influx of refugees on a large scale took place. It may be, however, noted that even before 1947 whenever there were communal riots in East Bengal (now Bangladesh), the Hindus generally took refuge in the State of Tripura. Such an influx had taken place after the Dacca communal riot in 1941. As a result, the Bengali Hindu population increased tremendously all over the State. After the partition in 1947, many Muslims also left Tripura for the newly created East Pakistan resulting in the decrease of the number of Muslim population in the State.

The decadal variations in population in Tripura since 1901 are given below for ready reference in table 4.2 :

From the table 4.2 it is clear that the growth rate of population in Tripura was more or less stable and it reflected the trends of natural growth. From 1911 to 1951 the range of variation of growth rate was 24.56 per cent to 34.14 per cent but after the partition of the country and, particularly after the merger of Tripura with the Indian Union, the growth rate was abnormally high. In 1961, the growth rate was as high

TABLE 4.2
Decadal Variations in Population

State	Year	Persons	Decade variation	Percentage decade variation
	1901	1,73,325	—	—
	1911	2,29,613	+ 56,288	+ 32.48
TRIPURA	1921	3,04,437	+ 74,824	+ 32.59
	1931	3,82,450	+ 78,013	+ 25.63
	1941	5,13,010	+ 1,30,560	+ 34.14
	1951	6,89,029	+ 1,26,019	+ 24.56
	1961	11,42,005	+ 5,02,976	+ 78.71
	1971	15,56,342	+ 4,14,337	+ 36.28
	1981	20,53,058	+ 4,96,716	+ 31.91

(*Sources* : Census of India)

as 78.71 per cent. Of course, the overall growth rate of population during the decade 1961-1971 works out to 36.28 per cent and whereas, the growth rates for the rural and urban areas (unadjusted) are 34.16 per cent and 57.64 per cent respectively. It may be noted that generally, growth rate of population is affected by three demographic factors, birth, death and migration. But in Tripura, the above abnormal growth rate during 1951-1961 was particularly on account of heavy influx of refugees from East Pakistan (now Bangladesh). No other State or territory in India had to accept about double the original population for settlement within its borders in such a short period of time. Mention may be made that the Maharaja of Tripura had a Relief and Rehabilitation Cell under the Revenue Department during the Raipur Communal riot in Dacca district of undivided Bengal in 1941 and Noakhali riot in 1946. After Noakhali riot, the Relief and Rehabilitation Cell was converted into a separate department as the Relief and Rehabilitation Department in the later part of the year 1948. The Government of India also sanctioned the Directorate of Rehabilitation in 1950 when a sudden influx of refugees took place after the great riot of 1950 in East Pakistan.

In this context, it may also be stated that Tripura kings from the very early times encouraged the immigration and settlement of the Bengali Hindus in Tripura. In fact the Tripura State Administration was for all practical purposes run and managed by these Bengali Hindus. The Maharajas of Tripura might have been motivated by two primary reasons viz., that such a migration of the Bengali Hindu would certainly augment the financial resources of the State by giving land holding rights to them. Secondly, the Maharajas were in favour of such migration because they thought that contact with these people would produce cultural enlightenment amongst the tribals. Thus, immigration and settlement of the Bengali Hindu is primarily responsible for the present population ratio of the tribals and the non-tribals in this State.

Now, due to direct and indirect contact with advanced alien culture, and more particularly with the Bengali Hindu culture of the plains, it has been noticed that the traditional tribal culture has largely undergone changes to such an extent that most of the tribes have almost lost their individualities or identities or are on the verge of losing the same.

The Hinduism and Tribes

It is quite well known that culture flows in a particular pattern from one community to another and this flow of cultural elements has always been from the materially superior people to the inferior ones. Or, this may be put in the other way, namely that the materially backward peoples always entertain or nourish or hanker after elevating their socio-economic position by assimilating or borrowing or adopting cultural traits from the more advanced peoples. Sometimes, it has been noticed that serious efforts are being made to get themselves fully absorbed within the fold of such a superior cultural community or communities. Here mention may be made that the assimilation of the Hindu cultural elements and pursuance of the Hindu ways of life by the tribes of Tripura has been a long drawn process. There is hardly any evidence of any kind of conscious efforts on either side, that is, the Hindus or the tribals. For the assimilation of the tribal people or for their entrance within the Hindu fold, the only instance of a deliberate attempt of denying tribal affiliation by the tribes of Tripura is to return themselves as Hindus during the Census enumerations. But this was also done without changing the tribal names as such. There is nothing wrong on the part of the tribal communities to return themselves as Hindus because of the very fact that there exists hardly any fundamental difference between the tribal religion and popular Hinduism. But the return of the tribals as Hindus does not necessarily deprive them of the tribal origins and tribal cultural organisation. This naturally raises a question as to how, and to what extent the tribes of Tripura adapted or borrowed or assimilated the Hindu ideas and ways of life as to call themselves Hindus ? One positive answer is that such an assimilation was the result of a natural process of adaptation or assimilation of the culture of a materially, economically and culturally superior people. These peoples are indeed the Hindus of the Plains and also those living in the peripheries of the State of Tripura. Even the contact between the Bengali Hindus and the tribal people which resulted in assimilation of the cultural traits of the former by the latter has been very slow and a longdrawn-out process. This becomes evident from a study of the history of the migration and settlement of the Bengali Hindus in Tripura.

Patronising Bengali Settlements

It may be noted that there have been deliberate attempts on the part of the tribal Kings of Tripura to encourage or patronise the settlement of the Bangali Hindus in the State. This encouragement was made by the Kings more particularly to obtain their active help and co-operation in running the administration and also in carrying out developments in the tribal areas. Not only that, the Kings themselves became very much engrossed in patronising Bengali learning and cultural attainments, and they themselves were fully infused with the Bengali culture. Such attempts by the tribal Kings of Tripura were not certainly made to Hinduize the tribal people, but to run the administration and carry-out development projects. This venture of the Kings of Tripura, however, bore fruitful results in the establishment of a very close and intimate contact between the tribal peoples and the Bengali Hindus. In support of this statement, mention may be made of the ruling chieftain of Tripura viz., Ratna-pha (15th century) who for the first time introduced the Bengali population in Tripura. It is important to note that the king was living in exile at the court of the Muslim King of Gouda (Bengal). He made friendship with that Muslim ruler. Subsequently, with the help of Pathan soldiers of the Sultan, he ascended the throne of Tripura. Now, as a mark of gratitude Ratna-Pha sent presents to the Sultan of Gauda. These presents included elephants and a highly priced ruby. Being greatly satisfied with these presents, the Sultan conferred the title of *Manikya* upon Ratna-pha.[1]

Royal Patronage to Bengali

It is said that Ratna Manikya settled thousands of the Bengali Hindu families in the Tribal areas of Tripura. This very settlement ensured a close contact of the Bengali Hindus with the Tripura rulers and the tribal people. Again, *Dharma Manikya* (1431-1462) the first great king of Tripura, was indeed a great patron of the Bengali learning and literature. It is under his patronage and direct encouragement that the *Rajmala* or the chronicles of the Kings of Tripura was composed in Bengali language. Not only that he also took steps for the permanent settlement of the Brahmins in different parts of the State and he himself became a devout follower of Hinduism.[2] The next King of Tripura was *Dhanya Manikya* (1490-1515) who was also a great patron of Bengali language. He caused many Sanskrit Texts like the *Jyotish Ratnakar* and the *Utkal-Kanda-Panchali* translated into Bengali. He also built several Hindu temples and employed the Bengali artists for making images of the Hindu deities.[3] Besides, an arch like big slab of stone bearing inscriptions speaks of the relics of another temple built by *Maharaja Vijoymanikya* in the Saka Era 1470. This slabstone has been found in the Maharani village of Udaipur sub-division. It was dedicated to the great

God Vishnu, by the royal couple. A temple of *Kali* was also built by Kalyan Manikya, though completed in 1662, thirty years after his death.[4]

Bengali as State Language

Not only that the tribal Kings of Tripura became Hindus, constructed Hindu temples and made settlements of the Bengali Hindus in different parts of the State, but also encouraged the Bengali language and literature. Most significantly, the Tripura Kings adopted Bengali as the State language. It is, however, difficult to state exactly the date when Bengali was made the State language. In this context, a reference may be made to the oldest available coins of the Tripura Kings bearing legends inscribed in Bengali script. All old *Sanada* and inscriptions are also found in Bengali language. Here, a particular mention may be made of the *Ayma-Sanad*, issued by Kalyan Manikya in the year 1659.[5] Again, the *Brahmottar-Sanad*, inscribed on a copper plate, was issued by the King Govinda Manikya in the year 1660. Thus, it Could be said that by about the 15th Century, the Bengali language established itself fully in the Tripura Court and it was made a State language. Even the Kings of Tripura issued postal stamps bearing legends in Bengali.[6] All these certainly speak about the extent to which Bengali was patronised and accepted in all administrative matters of Tripura.

Patronage to Western Education

The subsequent Kings of Tripura were also enlightened and well educated patronising the cause of education and spread of learning. From the second half of the 19th century Birchandra Manikya advocated the cause of Western education and undertook necessary steps and made arrangements for imparting Western education to the princess and members of the royal family. But more significantly, he also made arrangements for imparting lessons in Bengali to the tribals. The King himself was a man of literary genius and is credited with the composition of several poetical works in Bengali like the *Uchhvas*, *Akalkusum*, *Sohag* and *Prem-Marichika*.

Maharaja and Tagore

The most noteworthy event during the rule of the Maharaja Birchandra Manikya is, however, his association with the illustrious Bengali Poet Rabindranath Tagore. Being a lyrical poet himself the Maharaja could discover the genius of Rabindranath as a poet of great merit when the latter was only 22 years old. Rabindranath himself wrote : "His (Maharaja's) discerning eyes could divine an image of the future even in that immature start of my writings and had prompted him to honour me as a poet".[7] Next to Birchandra Manikya his son Radha Kishore Manikya continued also close contact with the poet Rabindranath who himself admitted that by saying, "... to him I was more than a poet—a friend and a brother". After, Radhakishore Manikya, Birendra Kishore Manikya and his successor, the last ruling prince, were also great pattrons of Bengali art and literature and all throughout maintained close contact with great poet who was highly honoured and respected by them.

Partition and Refugees

Thus, it is clear that all throughout the history of Tripura, the Kings not only patronised Bengali culture and religion and made settlements for the Bengalees, but also extended all sorts of active help and co-operation for their betterment and well-being. In this connection a particular reference may be made to the large scale influx of the Bengali Hindus from the neighbouring areas after the partition of Bengal in 1947. The Tripura King did never make any attempt to stop this influx of the Bengali Hindus. On the other hand he extended all Governmental help and co-operation for their settlements. Tripura also acceeded to the Indian Union on August 13, 1947. This accession produced a great impact on the Bengali Hindus of the neighbouring areas who on a large scale were encouraged to migrate to Tripura for their permanent settlement. The plain lands of Tripura came to be gradually occupied by the Bengali Hindus who became henceforth the permanent settlers of Tripura.

The Bengali Hindus who took refuge in Tripura were also largely employed in different capacities by the Kings for running the administration. In Tripura administration, the Ministers, the Advisers etc. and even the clerical staff or subordinate staffs became thereby predominantly Hindu. Again, after the partition of the country, the Bengalees not only settled in the plains, but even in the tribal areas where they engaged themselves in agricultural and other economic pursuits. In fact, it is now very difficult to find out any place in Tripura where no Bengali Hindus could be found.

Impact of Accession

Thus, for years together, and particularly from 1947, the Bengalees have been living in Tripura as the close neighbours of the tribal communities. In such a situation, the inflow of the Bengali cultural elements into the tribal ways of life and thought is quite inevitable and as a result of which, the tribal peoples of Tripura have adopted the Bengali Hindu ways of life and thought. This impact has transformed the tribal life-patterns to such an extent that these hilly peoples are now gradually losing their separate identity. This becomes evident from an analysis of the results of the impact of the Bengali culture on different aspects of tribal life in Tripura.

Changes in Modes of Production

While dealing with the economic life-patterns of the tribes, it has been found out that they were primarily food-gathering people living on gathering of forest produces and hunting animals and on a little fishing in the nearby catchments or rivulets. Besides these primary economic pursuits chopper, sickle, axe, hoe etc., which have been found to be more effective than their traditional tools. These adapted or borrowed material equipments gave stimulus for changing their economic activities and accordingly their modes of production also have undergone revolutionary changes. The introduction plough for cultivation revolutionised their food producing activities. The result was the change over to plough cultivation and the shift of settlements from the hilly areas to the plains. Further, it is because of plough cultivation that the quantum of food production increased considerably and the economic affluence emanating from it affected other aspects of their life as well. The traditional tribal tools and weapons have been replaced and all sorts of taboos relating to making and using of these tools have been given up. As for instance, taboos on weaving by man and on basket making by woman are no more strictly observed. On the otherhand, as a result of the introduction of metal made pots and utensils, mill made clothes, etc. the traditional arts and crafts are dwindling. Only a few of the different tribes are now found today engaged in their own tribal arts and crafts. Alongwith these changes, there has been an ever growing demand for more and more lands in the plains for plough cultivation. This has again brought about transformation in their settlement pattern and the construction of their houses. On the whole, the aforesaid changes in the modes of production of food-grains entirely have transformed the tribal life-patterns.

Changes in Social Life-patterns

With the changes in the modes of production and other economic activities, the social life-patterns of the tribals have also undergone consequential transformation in all aspects. Remarkable changes have taken place in preparation and consumption of food articles, dress and ornaments, customs and manner which are all being fashioned after the Bengali Model. The traditional marriage system, family organisation and social relationships have all changed both in their nature and character. The most popular traditional method of acquiring a mate amongst the tribals was the marriage by service which is corollary to the marriage by purchase i.e. by purchasing the bride. Presently, a good number of tribals do not usually take recourse to this method of acquiring a mate. On the otherhand, the order has reversed in the sense that now-a-days an ideal groom is adjudged on his academic attainments and on the basis of his capabilities for earning. Naturally, a service holder or a professional one is a much sought-after groom. The result has been the replacement of bride-price by groom price which is a general practice amongst the Bengali Hindus. Amongst the tribals of today, a Government employee is on great demand, and naturally so the father of such a prospective groom extracts cash money and even moveable or immovable properties from the brides' parents.

The position of the married women in the household has also changed considerably. Previously a tribal woman enjoyed sufficient liberty in regard to domestic works, marital separation, visits to the parents house etc. But now-a-days, she has been reduced to a subordinate position under the complete authoritative domination of her husband as in a Bengali family. Alongwith this, the traditional joint-family has disintegrated and presently an individual family has become the normal unit. It implies that coming into contact with the non-tribals, the tribals have now become more individualistic and the joint ownership of property and communal activities have today little role to play in their social behaviour patterns.

Growth of Class Distinction

It is again important to note that previously there was no class distinction or any kind of differentiation amongst the tribal communities but now because of new modes of production and other economic activities, class differentiation has become very marked in the tribal society. As for instance, the Government servants and the high ranking officers, if any, amongst the tribes have formed a class by themselves. This class is now considered as superior to all others because of their academic attainments and economic affluence. The second class consists of those who are wage-earners or working as labourers under different agencies. Three factors are involved in the emergence of this class stratification viz., education, employment and economic affluence. Above all, economic affluence is considered to be the only criterion or determining factor for any class affiliation. The members of such classes are also conscious of their respective positions, and generally speaking, their marital unions and other social relationships are also being restricted amongst the members of each of these classes. It is, however, to be noted that these classes have not yet turned to become endogamous units, but these are likely to be so in future as is happening amongst the peoples belonging to Scheduled Castes of the Hindu community. Besides, the aforesaid superior classes there are two others : the first one adhering to new economic pursuits of food producing by plough cultivation instead of *Jhum* cultivation and the second one living in isolated hilly areas and pursuing strictly their own traditional life-patterns, and as such, they live in abject poverty.

These are the four classes that can be distinguished amongst the tribes of Tripura today. It implies that class stratification in the tribal society has just started and naturally so, a kind of class conflict is likely to be the inevitable result. In fact several instances of such class conflict have been observed by the author during investigations in the field. But these class differentiations are, however, more glaring between the rich and the poor, the former representing the three upper classes and the latter, the last one. This class discrimination is likely to result not only in creating class conflicts, but also emergence of caste differentiations as to be found amongst the Bengali Hindus of the plains.

Change in Religious Beliefs

Similar changes are also witnessed in religious beliefs and practices of the tribes of Tripura resulting from the same contact with the Bengali Hindus of the plains. It does not however, mean that the tribes have totally given up their own traditional tribal religious behaviour. Apart from the tribal religious rites and practices, the tribal communities have adapted many elements of popular Brahmanism including the worship of some prominent Brahmanical deities like *Durga*, *Chandi*, *Saraswati*, *Luxmi*, *Mahadeva*, etc. Those who have adopted such worships of the Hindu deities have gone to the extent of having individual family worship of some minor deities like *Saraswati*, *Luxmi* and others. The images of these deities are purchased from the local markets and even the non-tribal Brahmin priests are being engaged to officiate. But in case of worship of major deities like *Durga*, *Kali*, etc. they simply participate in communal worships organised by the Bengali Hindus and in certain cases they also make contributions towards their expenses. It has not been very difficult on the part of the tribal peoples to accept the worship of these deities because of the very fact that all these deities were originally tribal in origins and it is only in a subsequent period that they have been Brahmanised. It is interesting to note that not only in religious behaviour patterns, but also in regard to philosophical outlooks and beliefs, the tribals have been able to think and visualise many philosophical concepts borrowed from popular Hinduism. As for instance, they now firmly believe in the theory of *karma*. They also believe that as a result of performing good and benevolent deeds during the life in this world the soul after death takes resort to the heavenly abode or *Swarga* which is also taken to be the abode of the deities. On the otherhand, by doing evil deeds the soul undergoes sufferings in the hell or *Naraka* i.e. the abode of the evil spirits. All these ideas are commonly prevalent amongst the general Hindus as well. Thus, the present position of the tribal religion is the synthesis of tribal religious beliefs and practices with those borrowed or adapted from Hinduism.

Impact of Modernisation

At present due to impact of modernisation, the tribal behaviour patterns have also changed considerably. Today, there is hardly any area which may be described as absolutely isolated because of the development of the modern means of communication, improved transport system and wide extent of Governmental interference in every aspect of life. It may be noted, in this context, that with the independence the National Government has been making every effort to develop all sorts of communications, linking the most impregnable areas with other parts, and as a result the tribes all over the State have come into direct contact with all sorts of peoples in and outside Tripura. Besides, the tribals living even in the remote areas are now coming into direct contact with the Government officials who include peoples from different parts of the country. The State Government at the same time is making every effort to extend all welfare and development activities even to the most interior regions. Under the changed circumstances following from direct governmental interference, the tribals have now become more and more secured in their respective settlements or villages. Previously, each tribal village used to be fortified or properly defended against all kinds of external dangers including inroads by other tribal peoples. As a result, the village solidarity and discipline which have been the key-note of the tribal ways of life have now lost its utility.

The easy means of communication and transport facilities have also largely affected the social life-patterns of the tribal peoples. The movement of the tribals has increased considerably. Now they move about from place to place in search of jobs, more particularly to work as labourers under contractors. But such works are primarily seasonal. In other lean months, the tribals are to lead an idle life without any earnings whatsoever. On the otherhand, the workers while engaged in far away villages under the contractors cannot take their families with them. Consequently, their family life has started disintegrating. Such works have again offered ample opportunities to the tribals for mixing freely with other non-tribals and they have been placed in a more favourable position to adopt many elements of other cultures.

It is evident from the above analysis that there has taken place a natural transition from the tribal life-pattern to modern ways of life and thought. This has been all due to the peaceful penetration of the Bengali Hindu cultural elements into the tribal arena. There was no deliberate attempt to integrate or assimilate the tribal people of Tripura within the Hindu fold, rather the tribes of their own accord have started adopting Hindu ways of life as far as possible in order to elevate their own socio-economic position. This has been all due to the natural flow of culture from a materially superior people to an inferior one. It is true that as a result of contact and cultural advancement the progress of the tribals have been achieved but there is another side of the picture. This is a picture of untold sufferings and miseries caused by the large scale exploitation carried out by the non-tribal infiltrators. Many tribals lost their holdings including agricultural lands their basic subsistence econoomy. Despite their cultural upbringing and transitions, the tribes of Tripura are now subjected to abject poverty. Everywhere the picture is a grim one. Everywhere the tribal peoples are ill-fed, ill-clothed and suffer from all sorts of miseries caused by both natural and human agencies.

It may also be noted that even a few years ago, the tribals

living in isolation had little knowledge about money as the medium of exchange. It is only in recent times that they have become conversant with the money economy and as such, regular trading is now quite well known to them. Such a great transition from a simple barter economy to money economy of trading has been brought about by several factors the most important of which appears to be the impact of contact with the peoples of the plains who are well conversant with money economy from a pretty long time. Secondly, the wide circulation of coins and their market value in relation to all economic pursuits have made the tribals gradually acquianted with the money economy and realised its utility as a medium of exchange. Thirdly, the transition from Jhum-cultivation to settled agricultural life has also brought about significant changes in both economic and social behaviour patterns of the tribals. The settled agricultural life created the utmost need of money economy because of the very fact that all equipments relating to agricultural operations are to be purchased mostly by money. Fourthly, the settled agricultural life and contact with the more advanced peoples of the plains also brought about great changes in the socio-economic life patterns of the tribals of Tripura.

Money Economy and the Growth of Market

The above factors have prompted the tribals to earn money for purchasing their needs. So, a tendency developed amongst them to produce more and more cash crops. They are now not satisfied simply by producing food-grains for their own consumption only. They now have engaged themselves in producing cash crops e.g., jute, rice, cotton both in jhum and ploughed fields. These crops are sold in the market and money thus earned is spent for purchasing tools, implements, ornaments, oil and all other requisites. In this connection Hunter (1876) observes "Jute was now not at least a cash crop produced by the Jhumias. It is quite likely that jute cultivation might have been a latter introduction, perhaps by the peoples of the plains. When the Jhumias found that jute thus produced can earn more cash crops than any other crop they also began to cultivate Jute".[8] All these crops and jungle products are generally marketed in the local markets. Sometimes, even brokers or traders purchase their produces from the tribal villages and these middlemen sell these purchased goods to the traders for export. Generally, the tribals carry their cash products to the markets for selling and purchasing their necessities. Of course, during the harvesting season, traders from the plains are in the habit of gathering at some fixed places where the tribal Jhumias would come along with their *Kharas* or baskets laden with articles to be bartered. Such a small gathering of purchasers gradually multiplied and become concentrated at one fixed placed which is called by the tribals as 'hat' or market. It may be noted in this context, that the tribals live in isolated and inaccessible hill areas causg a great amount of risk and inconvenience in respect of oving up and down with heavy loads, and as such, the question of attending any daily market from distant places does not arise. Landscape is largely responsible for the growth of periodic markets, mostly weekly in nature in the tribal areas. It may also be noted that the markets are usually organised on a rotation basis i.e., holding of markets at different places one after another. This is done to facilitate the visit of the traders at different places on the scheduled days. Previously, markets used to meet only in the morning and break away by noon in order to facilitate the return of the *Jhumias* to their respective homes before dusk, but now-a-days, the number of markets have increased and markets are located even in the hilly areas. As a result, the *Jhumias* can easily attend markets more frequently and conveniently. Accordingly, the scheduled time for holding a market has been also altered. A market is now held even in the afternoon and breaks at dusk. A characteristic feature of the tribal market is the absence of any permanent shop for stocking and selling goods. Only temporary thatched structures are raised for displaying articles to be sold.

In the absence of any cash crop at their disposal, the tribals collect forest produce for selling them in the market. Very often, the tribals are also found carrying domestic animals and birds like *Tak* (cock), *Oak-bacha* (pig) etc., to the nearby market for selling them.

Development of Transport

Another factor which has contributed much towards the break up of the isolation of the tribal economy is the opening-up of the aboriginal forest lands by means of transport and communications. Departmental working of forests and the needs of administration has hastened the development of transport since independence. Such development of transport has not only increased import and export trade of the region but also helped the growth of village and weekly markets. Forest roads and foot tracks have rendered many areas accessible to trade. As a result, the monopoly of the trade-money-lender and contact with the markets have changed the primitive character of agriculture as well as forest work. Now, under the new circumstances, the tribal Jhumias cultivate or collect not what they need for themselves but what satisfies the demand of the market or the itinerant trader. This has led to commercialisation of Jhumia agriculture. Again, the social effects of modern transport on Jhumias' life are also not less significant. Road construction and repair necessitate the movement of labour from one place to another since the work is of a seasonal character. The aboriginal workers cannot take their families to the spot of the work. This results in the temporary break-up of the Jhumia family. Tribal labourers being away from their homes and mixing freely with other tribals and non-tribals begin to neglect the conventional tribal code of social life. On the other hand, enforcement of Government laws and the detection of violation has become possible due to the development of transport. As a result, the tribals' faith on their traditional customs and institutions or in other words the collective tribal life is giving way to official fiats.

Exploitation of Forests

Again, the extension of forest operations to the remotest corner of the hill forests has brought the tribal people within its orbit. The departmental working of forests and contractor's operations are making these people familiar with the modern technique of forest exploitation. Now, a good number of tribals have learnt the use of saw machines.

They have also come to know the commercial values of certain forest products. Here mention may be made of Benchmark Survey conducted by the Tribal Welfare Department in 1978. According to the Benchmark Survey Report, the collection of forest products by the tribal Jhumias for sale is one of the important economic activities of about 70 per cent of the 2013 sample Jhumia families.[9] It is also reported that one hundred per cent of the Jhumia families collect bamboo, firewood and sungrass from forests for their own use and their average annual value amount to Rs. 185, Rs. 200 and Rs. 154.05 respectively.[10] It is interesting to note that, in contrast, non-traditional activities connected with forest resources seem to yield a higher level of income to the sample Jhumia families. According to the recent survey report, about 96 per cent of the Jhumia households earn incomes from wage employment, the average annual income of the sample Jhumia families from this source being Rs. 1790.50. The main source of wage employment of the Jhumias being the Forest Department which provides employment to a large number of Jhumias in development works. Besides, Forest Department, wage employment is also provided to the Jhumias by forest traders for the extraction of timber, firewood, bamboo, etc. Horticulture and plantations also provide employment to 3.9 per cent and 2.9 per cent of the sample Jhumia households and yield an average annual income of Rs. 452 and Rs. 400.05 respectively.[11] It is now clear from the above report that non-traditional activities connected with the forests have assumed importance in the economic life of the Jhumias of Tripura.

There is no doubt that Jhuming as a system of agriculture is the transitional stage from hunting and gathering to settled cultivation. Such system cannot survive in the long run because of the fact that increase of population in the absence of abundant supply of land is bound to shorten the cycle of Jhuming, bringing about continuous deterioration in soil fertility and ecological changes. It is also a fact that the population sustaining capacity of land under shifting cultivation is incredibly low. The studies conducted in the Philippines, Gambia, Malawi and Zambia including a few in India (Bose

1967 ; Ganguly 1969 and Saha, 1970) reveal that land carrying capacity under Jhuming is very low. It has been estimated that in Tripura, the population sustaining capacity of land under shifting cultivation is six persons per sq. km supposing 50 per cent of the areas amenable to the shifting cultivation.[12] According to Dr. Ganguly (1968), here in Tripura, a particular plot of land is Jhumed only once and then left fallow for about ten years for regeneration of forests. Hence, cultivation factor under Jhuming is 11. Dr. Ganguly further observes that in Tripura every year approximately 20,235 hectares of land is Jhumed which means that this form of cultivation can support about 2,200 souls only.[13] This shows the utter inadequacy of the system today.

The First Jhumia Settlement Attempt

Now, with the background of above information it is quite logical to replace this wasteful system of agriculture. Late Maharaja Bir Bikram Kishore Manikya Bahadur (1923-47) in order to induce his tribal subjects viz., Puran Tipras, Noatias, Jamatias, Reangs and Halams to plough cultivation instead of Jhum cultivation, reserved a large fertile ploughable area by an order dated 20th *Bhadra*, 1341 T.E. (1931) and by a subsequent order dated 1st *Aswin*, 1353 T.E. (1943), the area was extended later. It has been estimated that in the first Jhumia settlement attempt (1930-31) an area of 11,000 drones i.e. 28,490 hectares in Khowai Sub-division, called Kalyanpur Reserve was set apart as reserved for the settlement of the Jhumias. In the next order, the total area reserved for this purpose was raised to 5,05,053 hectares and as a result, there was sharp rise in the area under cultivation.[14] Again, in order to develop the vast tracts of wild land and populate them, His Highness opened a new Department called the Immigration and Reclamation Department. Soon after the opening of this department vigrous attempts were made for the study of material conditions of various tracts of land awaiting development. Reclamation work commenced in Kulai Haor, Dhalai Valley of Kailashahar Sub-division and various other places and nearly 400 sq. miles of land were distributed amongst the immigrants. The Agricultural Department which was reorganised at the instance of His Highness took up the work of introducing superior quality of cotton, paddy, jute, tobacco, sugarcane and potato in the high lands and in the plains.

Motivation in Favour of Plough Cultivation

Circuit lectures against nomadic Jhuming and in favour of plough cultivation was arranged by the said department. As a further step, the department opened an enquiry office in a specially constructed shed right in the heart of Agartala Bazar to furnish people with all information regarding agricultural operation, seeds, appliances, plants and cattle diseases. But unfortunately, in spite of sincere efforts, the progress of the settlement was not satisfactory. This will be evident from the Administrative Report for 1937-40 : "Many families have since permanently settled in the Reserve area and taken to ploughing, though the area actually brought under cultivation during the period was not encouraging".[15] As regards the progress of the scheme, the Report says : "Survey operations were carried on in 1347 T.E. (1937) with the Reserve in respect of 125 drons and 8 kanis i.e., 803.2 acres of land. The total expenditure incurred in the year 1347 T.E. in furtherance of the scheme amounted to Rs. 1,239-10-9 pies only, there being no expenditure in the following years."[16]

It is thus clear from the above Administrative Report that the progress of the settlement till 1940 was not impressive. It is important to note that besides, the creation of Jhumias settlement, the King also followed a general policy of urging the Jhumias to take to settled plough cultivation. The Tenancy Act of the State gave a special incentive to plough cultivation. According to the section 57 of the Law of Landlord and Tenant, a tenant who accepts a lease for reclamation of the hilly lands by cutting jungles shall get remission of rent for three years from the date of lease.[17] Again, in order to check the evil consequences of Jhuming on Act relating to Reserve Forests was passed in 1297 T.E. (1887 A.D) for the first time by the State. Amongst other things, the Act also prohibited Jhuming within half a mile of the boundary line of reserved forests (Clause VI) and none could set fire in the hills which might affect reserved forests in any way (Clause IX).[18] The Act laid down heavy punishment for any infringement of the provisions of the law. Any person setting fire and by whom was caused any damage to the trees in the reserved forests was liable to rigorous imprisonment upto six months or a fine not exceeding one thousand rupees or both.[19] Such measures however, affected the liberty of the Jhumias to do Jhum anywhere they liked as before.

Najrana for Tribal Lands

The rulers of Tripura also encouraged large-scale immigration of cultivators and middle class cultured persons from the adjoining districts of Bengal to open out the way for general development and prosperity of the State. The actual intention and purpose of such settlement of land will be clear from excerpt from the proceedings of the *Shashan Sanmilani* of 1323 T.E. (1913 A.D) : "the system of permanent settlement should be continued. Instead of distributing small pieces of land large areas of 500 drons i.e., 3200 acres or more in one block should be given out in permanent settlement. This measure will lead to an increase in the number of rich and cultured persons as also of ordinary tenants. And if rich, wealthy and resourceful persons take such taluka (estates), then by their endeavour roads and other means of communication will be built up which will open out the way for general development and prosperity of the State."[20] As a result of the above measure the purpose of the rulers of Tripura, however, was fulfilled temporarily but that vitally affected the life-pattern of the Tribals. The immigrants began to grab land paying a nominal *njrana* (tribute) to the king and in the process met the folk in the interiors who were almost taken by surprise.

Inflow of Refugees

This influx greatly increased after the partition till the end of 1950, during which about 1,75,000 displaced persons crossed the border and come over to Tripura from the adjoining district now in Bangladesh. This inflow of refugees however, was checked to a considerable extent since 1958 when the Government announced its decision not to register immigration as displaced persons. Upto the above mentioned period 83,000 families consisting of 3,74,000 persons officially registered themselves as displaced persons from Bangladesh.[21] Of course, another wave of migration started from the middle of 1963 due to communal riots in Khulna, Jessore and other districts of Bangladesh. Again during Bangladesh liberation war thousands of refugees migrated to this land for shelter. This rehabilitation of refugees in the rural areas of Tripura completely shattered the remnents of isolation enjoyed by the tribals. Not only that, the marshy lands reclaimed for settling the refugees thus, resented in a further fall in the area available to the tribals to shift about for nothing.

It would be evident from the analysis of socio-economic life-pattern that the tribal economy has been throughout basically a primitive one. It is a simple economy based on procuring the primary needs of life, viz., food and shelter. For pursuing the aforesaid economic activities, the requisites were also very simple and small consisting of digging-sticks, bows and arrows, cutting tools, baskets etc. All these food gathering and food producing tools were made by the tribals themselves. Whatever, these people gathered and produced were consumed by them and as such, in all respects the tribal-economy were self-sufficient and self-contained. But the persistance or continuation of such an economy depends largely on the bountiful gift of nature. Presently, the landscape has been fast changing and the angry nature has been taking revenge on the very people whom it so long sustained and nursed.

Observation

It is because of the changing pattern of the landscape that the forest products are now becoming more and more scarce, hardly sufficient to meet the requirements of these peoples for their very subsistence. But not only nature is responsible for it, even the human agency largely contributed towards the scarcity of jungle productions available to the tribals. Constant felling of trees and clearance of jungles have driven out animals, and the availability of fruits, herbs and roots has become scarce. Again, as a matter of fact, the incipient Jhum-cultivation has also now become less fruitful. It is known that a *Jhum*-field cannot be subjected to continuous cultivation for years together, and as such, the Jhuming operation is to be shifted from one field to the another. Previously, there was no dearth of land for transformation into *Jhum*-fields, but at present, lands or forest areas are hardly available for the same and as a result Jhuming operation has become an impossibility. This problem has become more acute by the growth of population. No-availability of sufficient forest or *Jhum*-fields for producing their livelihood has been largely responsible for deterioration in their conditions day by day.

Fortunately, the tribal people found out alternative means of procuring their livelihood by taking recourse to more substantial and potential means of production, which they have borrowed and most successfully adopted to suit their own life patterns and means of subsistance. The fruitful results of plough-cultivation have become known to the tribals and the adoption of such cultivation has brought about revolutionary changes in the socio-economic life-patterns of the Jhumias. First, instead of nomadic or wandering tribal life subsisting on food-gathering and *Jhum*-cultivation, the tribal Jhumias have now largely become settled agricultural people. This nomadic incipient farming community has now become transferred into a firmly agricultural community. Secondly, the Jhumias used to produce only crops of their livelihood in the *Jhum*-field. But with the introduction of currency system and money economy, the whole life-pattern changed. They first started producing cash crops in the *Jhum*-fields and next even in the fields under plough cultivation. Thirdly, the settled agricultural life and plough cultivation have brought money economy followed by other consequential changes in the general life patterns of the Jhumias. Their needs for worldly maintenance and the craving for better and prosperous life after the plains people have encouraged the Jhumias more and more to produce cash crops to earn money and to meet their created demands. Fourthly, the settled agricultural life has also brought about baneful effects eating into the vitality and the very existence of the Jhumias. It may be noted that previously in times of any need, the tribals could borrow food grains from another family and the same could be returned in kind, but now, the situation has changed considerably. For each and everything the tribals are to take recourse to money transactions. In times of need, they are to borrow money to purchase food-grains and other necessities. The result has been disastrous. The Jhumia villages are now frequented by money-lenders who lend money on exorbitant interest and the amount is to be repaid in cash, not in kind. In the case of the failure of cash crops, such loans can hardly be re-paid and accordingly, the Jhumias have now become victims of these money-lenders. In fact, the Jhumias are now living in perpetual debt and poverty. For repaying loans, the Jhumias have to adopt the last resort of selling their agricultural lands to the money-lenders or to others. As a result, the Jhumias are being deprived of their agricultural land and other holdings as well. Besides, the partition of the country and the consequent refugee settlement all over the State made the agricultural land problems more and more acute. The refugees coming over to Tripura have purchased lands from the Jhumias of different tribal communities. Because of the abject poverty, the Jhumias also had no alternative but to sell them. Again, the exploitation of forests on modern lines has caused a fundamental change in the life-patterns of the Jhumia's freedom over forests and compelled them to give up traditional way of life. This is how the tribal people have been deprived of their forests, *Jhum*-fields and agricultural lands. Being divorced from their traditional life-patterns, and deprived of their acquisitions, many of the tribals have now been forced to become daily wage-earners working as casual labours in Government Forest Department or in any contractor's firms.

It is however, heartening to note that the State Government is determined to ameliorate the condition of the tribals and as such, certain Acts have been passed in regard to land-holdings. According to the laws enacted by the State Government, no land belonging to any tribal community can be purchased by any non-tribal person. Not only that, lands already sold out to such persons shall revert to the original owners who sold them. Thus, the Government is making all out efforts to make the Jhumias economically self sufficient but unfortunately the overall economic position of the Jhumias has not improved much. It would not be, however, inappropriate to say that their economy has not been improved to the desired level even after more than three and half decades of the attainment of independence.

REFERENCES

1. Chatterjee, S.K. : *J.R.A. S.B.* Vol. XVI, 1950, p. 216.
2. *Ibid.*
3. Menon p. 69.
4. *Ibid.*
5. *Ibid.*, p. 88.
6. *Ibid.*, p. 339
7. *Tripura Ties with Tagore* : Directorate of Education, Government of Tripura, Agartala, 1969, p. 17.
8. Hunter, W.W. : Statistical Account of Bengal, Vol. VI (Hill Tipperah) Calcutta, 1876, p. 503.
9. *Benchmark Survey Report.* Tribal Welfare Department, Government of Tripura, Agartala, 1978,
10. Banerjee, A. Dasgupta, Miss M. Roy O.P. : The Importance of Forests in the economic life of the Jhumias of Tripura. (The Article was submitted in the Seminar on Planning for Forestry Development in the North-Eastern Region, Agartala, 1984).
11. *Ibid.*
12, Jha, S.D. : *Shifting Cultivation in North-East India*, Shillong, 1976, p. 32.
13. Ganguly, J.B.: *Economic Problems of the Jhumias of Tripura* Calcutta 1969.
14. Menon, K.D. : *Tripura District Gazetteers,* 1975 Calcutta pp. 160-161.
15. *Administrative Report for 1937-40,* Government of Tripura, Section 176-178.
16. *Ibid.*
17. Ganguly, J.B. : *Economic Problems of the Jhumias of Tripura* Calcutta, 1969. p. 67.
18. *Ibid.*
19. *Ibid.*
20, *Ibid.*
21. *Ibid.*

FIVE

ADMINISTRATION AND INADEQUACIES OF SAFEGUARD

The policy of ancient Indian rulers about the tribal population had been that of respect for their traditions and institutions. The tribals also played a decisive role in determining the social complex of the society. The historical fact is that in the struggle for supremacy between the Brahmanism and the Buddhism, the Brahmans banked on the support of the powerful tribes like the *Sakas, Pallavas* by conferring on them, the status of Kshatriyas. Thus, a process of peaceful give and take policy was prevalent through the ages. This process, however, suffered a set back with the establishment of British Rule in India. They extended roads to the outlying tribal areas for their commercial and military interests. They also did not care at all about the development of the tribal economy. The tribals were exposed to exploitation by contractors, landlords and money-lenders. Naturally, the tribals were not happy with the encroachment. Their resentment took the shape of rebellions in the various parts of the country.

The first noteworthy rebellion which had great impact in formulating tribal policy by the British Government was that of the Malpaharias of Rajmahal hills 1772. Subsequent tribal the uprisings were : the mutiny of the Hos of Singbhum in 1831, Khond unrest in 1846, Santhal rebellion in 1885. In Tripura also, such uprisings had been voiced several times. The underlying causes of these uprisings were, however, deep dissatisfaction created among the tribal people against exploitation by their more advanced neighbours. The British Government adopted the policy of pacification through indirect rule. The traditional leaders of the Paharias were granted *Sanads* and annual payments. They, on their part were required to report all crimes in the villages under their control, use their influence to prevent any breach of peace and assist the authorities, when called upon to do so.[1] The tract was thus administered without any of the regular laws of the British Government.

It is interesting to note in this context that the phrase 'Tribal Areas' was first introduced by the Government of India Act, 1935, Section 311 (1), which defined them as "the areas along the frontiers of India or in Baluchistan which are not part of British India or of Burma or of any Indian State or of any foreign State. India together with all territories of any Indian ruler under the suzerainty of his Majesty, all territories of any Indian Ruler, the tribal area, and any other territories which His Majesty in council may, from time to time, declare to be part of India."[12]

The jurisdiction of His Majesty over the whole 'India' admits of no doubt in the 1935 Act. Again, Section 294 provided for the relation between the Governments of British Indian and Indian States being conducted by the foreign jurisdiction Act of 1890 and Section 8(1/e) of the same Act brought the 'tribal areas' under complete executive authority of the federation, discharged by the Governor-General, according to Section 11 (1) in his direction. The Governor-General might be advised, in this respect, according to sub-section 2 of the same section, by a Counsellor and might delegate the power, according to Section 123 (1) to a Provincial Governor, who is the agent of the Governor-General, would be acting in his discretion. The Constitutional assimilation of the 'tribal areas' with British India, was complete, though its special status was recognised.[3] However, the revised Foreign Jurisdiction order in council of the King, dated 18th March, 1937 excluded the 'Tribal areas in India' from the scope of Foreign Jurisdiction "without prejudice, however, to the validity of anything previously done thereunder".[4] A notification of the Government of India's External Department (No.1-IX), Dated 1st April, 1937 directed the Governor of Assam to discharge functions as the agent of the Governor-General of India in Council" and in relation to the tribal areas beyond the external boundaries of the province of Assam all functions hitherto discharged in and in relation to the said area by the Governor as the agent of the Governor-General in respect of the political control of trans-border tribes, the administration of the Assam Rifles and the Armed Civil Forces."[5]

Thus beyond the administered area, the British created a zone of 'political control' dating back to at least 1866. In the later years the area of political control progressively shifted to the inner hills as the horizons of the administration expanded step by step and finally, the Second World War appeared to have inspired a full-scale 'forward policy' on the tribal areas. On 23 October, 1943 the service of J.O. Mills, till then Secretary to the Governor, were placed "at the disposal of the Government of India for employment as Advisor for Tribal Areas and States of His Excellency the Governor of Assam".[6] The Secretarial functions in relation to the tribal areas continued to be disposed off by the Governor's Secretariat. The expansion of administration, however, did not proceed much because of the pressure of war and the impending British withdrawl.[7]

Subsequently, the transfer of power led to the abolition of the special Constitutional status of the tribal areas as the India (Provisional Constitution) order of 15th August, 1947 altogether dropped all references to 'tribal areas' discretionary powers of the Governor-General and Governors and distinction between 'India' and 'British India'. According to Sarin (1980) the repeals however, at once put their link with India on a doubtful footing. On 27 August, 1947, the Governor-General issued the Extra Provincial Jurisdiction Ordinance, with effect from 15th August, 1947 as issued by Government of India, indeed with retrospective effect, and calling the tribal areas on the frontiers of the Province of Assam as 'Assam Tribal Areas' (Ministry of

External Affairs and Commonwealth Relations—Notification No. 387 NEF, Gazette of India, Part I, 30 October, 1947).[8]

It would appear that though physically the tribal areas were made more accessible to the rest of the country, psychologically an image of their being different was gradually built up and administratively they were kept in isolation. In support of this contention reference may be made that in 1847 the Indian Legislature passed the Scheduled District Act, "whereby the local Government was empowered to declare in respect of the tracts. Specified in the Act what enactments were or were not in force and to notify the application with modifications or restrictions, if necessary, of any enactment in force at the time, in any part of British India."[9] It is to be noted that the above policy of keeping the tribal areas administratively separate continued in the Government of India Act, 1919 and the Government of India Act 1935.

According to the Act of 1919, the Governor-General-in-Council is empowered to declare any territory to be a backward tract and with the sanction of the Secretary of State to direct that the Government of India Act shall apply to the territory with such exceptions and modifications, as may be prescribed in his notifications. Thereafter, he may direct that any Act of the Indian Legislature shall not apply to the territory or shall apply with such exceptions and modifications as he may prescribe. Further, he may authorise the Governor-in-Council to issue similar directions in respect of the Acts of the Provincial Legislatures. The power of issuing regulations by executive orders in regard to these territories still remained.[10]

But however, the actual implementation of the 1919 Act did not follow a uniform pattern in all provinces. Surprisingly, it differed from province to province depending upon the strength of the nationalist movement and the orientation of the tribals themselves. Again, the Government of India Act of 1935 is more alarming in the sense that the policy of keeping the tribals isolated was further intensified through the provisions for delimitation of excluded and partially excluded areas under Section 92 of the Act. It has been stated that "no act of the Federal or Provincial Legislature applies to an excluded or to a partially excluded area, unless the Governor directs its application by notification. In applying any Act, the Governor may make such modifications or exceptions as he thinks fit. The Governor may take regulations for the peace and good Government of any such areas including regulation for the repeal or amendment of any existing Indian Law.[11]

After Independence

The above provisions of the Government of India Acts 1919 and 1935 were strongly opposed by the nationalist leaders on the ground that the provisions indicated a distrust about the goodwill and consideration of the politically conscious Indians about their tribal brethern problems. It has been stated in Article 339 of new Constitution that the President of India may at any time and shall at the expiration of ten years from the commencement of the Constitution by an order appoint a Commission to report on the administration of the Scheduled Tribes in Part A and Part B States. This provision, however, does not include the Part 'C' States, and Tripura was at that time included in that category. But subsequently, an amendment to this Article was made to cover the Scheduled Tribes of Part 'C' States as well. As a result, the State of Tripura was also covered by the provisions under Article 339. Besides, the Constitution has also made special provisions of safeguards for the Scheduled Castes and Scheduled Tribes. These provisions of safeguards were particularly made to facilitate the implementation of the Directive Principles of the State Policy as contained in Article 46 of the Constitution as : "The State shall promote with special care the educational and economic interests of the weaker sections of the people, and in particular of the Scheduled Castes and Scheduled Tribes, and shall protect them from social injustice and all forms of exploitation."

Further provisions have been made for banning forced labour and appointment of special officers for investigation into all matters relating to safeguarding the interests of the tribal people.[12] Besides under Articles 330, 332 and 334 of the Constitution provisions have been made for the reservation of seats for the tribals in the Parliament and State Legislature and that their claims for appointment in Public Offices are to be given preference too. In pursuance of the Article 335 of the Constitution a fair percentages of vacant posts are to be reserved and progressive measures are also to be undertaken for making the Scheduled Tribes qualified for such appointments.

Commission for Schedued Castes and Scheduled Tribes

As per Constitutional provisions, a Commissioner was appointed by the President of India to investigate into all matters relating to safeguarding the interests of the tribal people. The Commission started functioning from November 18,1950 under a Commissioner assisted by six Regional Commissioners with jurisdiction over 17 States.[13] The functions or duties of the Commission have been also clearly defined. The Commission is to investigate all matters relating to the safeguards provided under the Constitution and also to report directly to the President on the working and implementation of the Constitutional provisions made for the tribal peoples. Accordingly, the Commissioner for the Scheduled Castes and Scheduled Tribes submits an annual report each year to the President. This report is again subjected to discussions in the Parliament of India.

Dhebar Commission

Following the accession of the State to the Union of India in 1949, an administrator was appointed by the President of India as the Chief Commissioner of Tripura which was thence formed into part 'C' State and included in North-eastern Indian region. It is important to refer in this context that after the accession of the State to the Indian Union the Central Government appointed the Dhebar Commission in 1950 to examine the problems of the Scheduled Caste and Scheduled Tribe population of the country. Shri N.M. Patnaik, the then Chief Commissioner of Tripura submitted a note to the Commission stating that a specified area should be declared as reserved for the tribal people under Schedule V of the Constitution. The Dhebar Commission however, recommended inter-alia that Tribal Development Blocks might be set up as an experimental measure in tribal compact areas and if this measures failed to bring about any material improvement among the tribal people, measures under Schedule V might be given a trial.[14]

Administrative Reforms Commission

Besides Dhebar Commission, an Administrative Reforms Commission, was also set up under the Chairmanship of Sri K. Hanumanthaiah. The Commission after examining the above issues suggested that some compact tribal areas in the States like Manipur and Tripura might be specified and Tribal Councils set up there along with delegation of well defined administrative powers.[15] Shri Jawaharlal Nehru, the then Prime Minister of India also convened a national conference in 1952 to discuss problems affecting the Scheduled Castes and Scheduled Tribes population of the Country. In that conference Sri Dasarath Deb, the then Member of Parliament proposed that a definite area should be declared as reserved for the tribal people of Tripura. He said, "Some area or areas of Tripura shall have to be set aside for the tribals alone and no other person belonging to non-tribal communities should be allowed to settle there and this conference should take note that this is not a new idea at all."[16] Subsequently, the Tripura Rajya Gana Mukti Parishad in a memorandum submitted to the Prime Minister of India on September 10, 1955 stated, "the scramble for land in Tripura has reached such a point that it is no longer possible for the tribal Jhumias to find new lands for Jhuming nor are they in a position to retain their old Jhuming lands traditionally used for cultivation. So Government *Khaslands* around tribal habitations should be declared as reserved areas for rehabilitation of the tribal communities.[17]

Tribal Advisory Committee

As against this background the Commission for Scheduled Castes and Scheduled Tribes recommended the formation of Tribal Advisory Committee in the State of Tripura in 1956 for the first time. The Advisory Committee was formed with the Chief Secretary of the State as its Chairman with four officials and four non-officials as its members to advise the administration in carrying out the welfare activities amongst the tribals of Tripura. This Advisory Committee was reconstituted in 1959 and two more non-official members were included. In pursuance of looking after the communities of Tripura, the Parliament in 1960 passed, "The Tripura Land Revenue and Land Reforms Act' under Article 186 of the said Act, certain conditions have been laid down, which made the transfer of tribal land very difficult and more complicated. The Advisory Committee, on the expiry of its terms in June, 1962 was again reconstituted on the 23rd September, 1963 with the purpose of improving the prevailing conditions of the tribal communities of Tripura.

Tripura Land Revenue and Land Reforms Act

In January, 1972 Tripura became a full-fledged State. The Tripura Land Revenue and Land Reforms Act of 1960 was further amended in 1974 by laying more rigorous conditions in respect of the transference of tribal holdings. A third amendment of the said Act of 1960 was made in 1975. In this amendment Sections 107(A) to 107(E) have been inserted to safeguard the interest of the members of the tribal communities in respect of the transfer of tribal holdings. It contains clear provisions regarding sale or purchase of the tribal land. It has been laid down that if a member of any tribal community desires to sell his land, the first offer shall have to be made to his co-sharer and failing that, the offer may be made to the adjoining tribal land-holder. In the absence of any such tribal land-holder, the offer shall have to be made to any landless member of a Scheduled Tribe living in that area. Any transfer of tribal land in contravention of the provisions of the Act shall be void. But it is contended that the above Land Reforms Act and its subsequent amendment of 1974 were detrimental to the tribal interest. Because, among other things, the Land Reforms Act of 1960 also provided that a land transfer away from the tribals, needed the Collector's permission.[18] As a result of this provision it has been reported that a good number of tribals of Dashda of Kanchanpur area were uprooted from their own land and had sought shelter elsewhere. Secondly the 1974 amendment went further, requiring the restoration of tribal land alienated on or after 1st January, 1969 in contravention of the Act.[19] Thus the second amendment i.e. the 1974 amendment, in fact, virtually legalised transfers that had taken place before 1st January, 1969. Not only that, the progress of restoration of land had been distinctly very slow.

Autonomous Council

However, in accordance with the Constitutional provisions made for looking-after the interests of the tribal communities of Tripura, the Government of Tripura decided to set up an Autonomous Council to introduce internal autonomy in tribal compact areas and thereby protecting the socio-economic and cultural interests of the tribal population in Tripura. It has been felt that the above council should be set up in terms of Schedule VI of the Constitution and pending that it has been decided to establish the Autonomous District Council in terms of Schedule VII of the Constitution. Accordingly, the Tripura Tribal Areas Autonomus District Council Bill, 1979 was unanimously passed by the Tripura Legislative Assembly on March 23, 1979. The Bill includes provisions for the Constitution at Autonomous District Council consisting of the Tribal tehsils and villages, which shall deal with the following matters:[20] (a) Allotment and occupation or use of Scheduled Land or any other land which is covered by a reserve forest, (b) Management and control of any forest not being a reserved one, (c) Regulations in regard to Jhum or other kinds of shifting cultivation, (d) Dealing with any other matters relating to village and town administration and (e) Regulating and controlling money lending or trading within the State.

Though Autonomous District comprises areas from various administrative units in the State, there is, however, no provision for sub-autonomous district like a region as contained in the 6th schedule. The Act also envisages the Constitution of the Village Council endowed with powers to try certain civil cases or any other cases arising out of any bye-laws, regulations or rules in force in the Autonomous District as well as cases arising out of any bye-laws, regulations, offences or abettment thereof, which are not punishable with death, imrisonment for life or imprisonment for a term not exceeding six months and offences under section 379 and 380 of the Indian Penal Code, where the value of the stolen property does not exceed Rs. 5,000.[21]

It is, however, gratifying to note that during session of the Parliament (1984-85) the Constitution was amended unanimously for introducing the Schedule VI in Tripura. The main object behind the formation of the Autonomous District Council was to handover certain administrative and legal authority to the council in order to devote concerted attention to all aspects of cultural, social and economic improvement of the tribal people.

It is thus evident that the policy of the Central Government is to bring the Scheduled Tribes of the Union of India shoulder to shoulder with the advanced people for the purpose of doing away with all sorts of social and economic discrimination. This policy can be materialised only by adopting certain concrete steps and measures for the improvement of the condition of the tribal people. Now, a persual of the measures undertaken by the Government for improving the socio-economic conditions of the tribal people is absolutely necessary for a proper understanding of the problems of the Scheduled Tribes of Tripura.

It has already been pointed out that a provision has been made in the Constitution of India for the creation of the office of the Commissioner for Scheduled Castes and Scheduled Tribes to adopt certain concrete steps and measures for the improvement of the condition of the tribal people and also to supervise all activities of the State Governments in this regard. Every State of the Union shall accordingly submit an Annual Report containing all details about the measures undertaken and implemented by the State for the welfare and advancement of the Scheduled Tribes. The Commissioner includes such reports from each State in his Annual Report for submission to the President.

In respect of the State of Tripura, the picture presented by the Commissioner's Annual Reports regarding the Tribal peoples of the State is indeed appalling. It would be seen that in most of the years from 1955 till 1978, the State

Government of Tripura failed to submit Annual Reports in this respect to the Commissioner's office. It has been stated that information as wanted under different items were not available.[22] It implies that during this period no positive step was undertaken or done or achieved during this period.

There are, of course, some available reports regarding the progress of the Tribal Welfare Works in Tripura. An analysis of such reports may be made here under such headings as : (i) Jhumia Settlement i.e. the settlement of the shifting cultivators on agricultural land in the plains, (ii) Education i.e. measures taken by the State Government for the promotion of education or for the removal of illiteracy amongst the tribal peoples, (iii) Employment i.e., to what extent the tribals have been appointed in different offices, (iv) Housing schemes i.e. financial assistance given for constructing houses by the individual tribal families and (v) Welfare measures i.e. various measures so far adopted by the State Government for improving the socio-economic conditions of the tribal people and also for their overall advancement.

Jhumia Settlement

It is pertinent to mention that the national policy is to discourage shifting cultivation and to encourage plough cultivation for better agricultural production. The tribal shifting cultivators are no doubt very keen to adopt plough cultivation and accordingly necessary provisions had been made by the Central as well as by the State Government. In this respect it would be profitable to refer to the observations made by the Commissioner for Scheduled Castes and Scheduled Tribes as embodied in the Report of the Commissioner of 1959-60 ; "During my tours in Tripura, it was observed that the Jhumias were inclined to give up shifting cultivation gradually, provided that they were settled on good agricultural land......, I am glad to learn that the Union Administration have already suggested such a measure for weakening away the Jhumias from shifting cultivation." It was only in 1953-54 that the State Government submitted a scheme for granting-in-aid under Article 275(1) for the settlement of the Jhumias and an amount of Rs. 83,596 was allocated for the purpose.[23] However, the achievements of the Government regarding settlement of the Jhumias are tabulated year-wise as per data obtained from the various records.[24]

From the Table 5.1 it is evident that total number of Jhumia families settled so far (1984-85) in 45,091. In 1974-75 total allocation of fund for Jhumia by the State Government was Rs. 29.94 lakhs and expenditure made during the same year was Rs. 28.90 lakhs. But unfortunately allotted by the Centre during that period. In the subsequent year i.e. in 1975-76, although Centre made allocation for this purpose but the amount was too meagre even in comparison to State's allotment. Again, in most of the years, during the period from 1974-75 to 1984-85 the State Government failed to spend the total money as allotted for the settlement of the Jhumias. In 1974-75, under item No. 2 it appears that the total fund allotted for the settlement of Jhumia was Rs. 29.94 lakhs and the amount spent for the same purpose was Rs. 28.90 lakhs but the number of benefited was 4249 whereas in the subsequent year more fund was allotted both by the Centre as well as by the State, the amount being Rs. 39.51 lakhs but the number of families benefited was only 2482 i.e. about half of the the number of the previous year's physical achievement. Another interesting feature is that according to the State Report on Tribal Benchmark Survey in Tripura (1978) there are 23,292 number of tribal households who are completely dependent on Jhuming and about 23,565 number of households are partly dependent on Jhuming but from the above table it appears that by 1984-85 about 45,091 families already benefited by the *Jhumia* settlement programme scheme. Thus, the figures relating to the number of Jhumias seems to be anomalous. The common experience is that after receiving aid from the Government every adult member of a Jhumia family gets separated from the parent unit, move elsewhere and registers his name as a Jhumia for receiving further monetary aid from the Government. As a result, the number of Jhumia families almost remain as static. Hence till now due to lack of scientific approach the true picture of *Jhumia* settlement is not coming out.

Again, from the consideration of the allocation of funds and

TABLE 5.1

Jhumia Settlement

Year	Allocation of funds (Rs. in lakhs)		Expenditure (Rs. in lakhs)		Physical achievement No. of families	
	State	Centre	State	Centre	State	Centre
1	2	3	4	5	6	7
1974-75	29.94	—	28.90	—	4249	—
1975	29.51	10.00	29.74	10.00	1982	500
1976	35.00	32.92	29.31	32.92	2932	1496
1977	35.75	65.00	35.30	64.91	3247	3085
1978	40.60	79.43	38.11	78.97	2921	3536
1979	31.80	88.95	30.98	88.72	1397	4755
1980	40.22	61.33	36.61	60.05	1838	2973
1981	55.28	25.16	54.69	25.16	2380	1171
1982	19.30	28.17	17.83	27-50	915	1114
1983	14.30	22.90	13.41	22.80	666	1155
1984	20.80	21.21	20.71	21.20	587	818

total amount spent for the purpose, it would appear that little progress has been achieved in weaning away the shifting cultivators and settling them on plain lands for plough cultivation. Out of the total number of 5,83,920 tribal people about 2,25,000 have been so far resettled. This is certainly not a satisfactory achievement in respect of the resettlement of the *Jhumias* on the plain lands for plough cultivation.

Education

As regards education, no serious attempt has been made so far to impart the same to them. The tribes of Tripura like other tribes have no script of their own and naturally the question of imparting any formal education through their own mother tongue does not arise. The *Maharajas* did pay little attention to educating the tribal people. Not only that even little provision was not made for the spread of education within the State amongst all sections of the people.

The Bengal Administration Report for the year 1874-75 shows that the prospect of education in Tripura was far from bright and almost no attention was paid to its improvement. The report observes that with an estimated population of nearly 75,000 souls, there are about 103 boys undergoing instructions at the two existing schools.[25] The report adds that the number of schools on 31st March, 1879 was 25 and the number of pupils attending schools was 700. Of the 700 pupils 30 are the sons of 'Thakurs' or royal families, 52 Tipperahs, 232 Manipuris[26] and the remainder 388 Bengali Hindus and Muslims. However, it has been found that in 1931-32 under the State Act-2 compulsory primary education was introduced. But unfortunately, the scope of the Act was confined only to the municipal area of State capital Agartala covering the students of only four primary schools for all practical purposes. The following Table 5.2 shows the extent of educational facilities in the pre-independence period.[27]

It is evident from the Table 5.2 that educational facilities during the Kingly reigns was not at all adequate. In 1907-08 the number of schools was 137 in the whole State and the number of pupils going to schools was 4,011, the percentage of primary children to total school going children being 18.5%.

TABLE 5.2

Educational Facilities before Independence

Year	No. of Schools	No. of pupils	Percentage of primary children to total school going children
1907-08	137	4,011	18.5
1916-17	125	4,842	16.5
1926-27	139	4,215	10.6
1936-37	111	5,110	7.9
1943-46	123	5,115	7.9

Strangely enough the number of schools decreased in 1936 and the trend continued till 1946. It is thus obvious that in the pre-independence period educational facilities even at the primary stage did not increase in proportion to the increase of State population.

However, after the merger of the State with the Union of India little attention was paid for spreading education at different levels. In 1951, the literacy was 15.5 per cent, the total number of literates being 1,00,084. In 1961, the rate of literacy rose to 20.2 per cent and finally according to the Census Report of India, the literacy was 42.12 in 1981.[28]

It may be noted in this context that although there was increase in enrolment of students in all types of educational institutions, the non-admission of backward classes particularly Scheduled Castes and Scheduled Tribes was very spectacular and prominent till 1957.[29] It is, however, to be borne, in mind that national policy is to encourage and spread education amongst the weaker sections and it is only by spreading education that improvement or advancement could be ushered in amongst them. But unfortunately, it appears that no significant result has yet been achieved in this regard. It also appears that as yet no special or separate arrangements have been made for imparting any formal education to the tribal peoples alone. Nor any voluntary organisation, has come forward to set up any educational institution of any standard

TABLE 5.3

Tribals and Spread of Education

Educational Standard	Year	Total No. of students attending	No. of Scheduled Tribe students attending	No. Scheduled Caste students attending
1	2	3	4	5
Primary stage (from class I-V)	1987	3,58,590	1,05,700	66,380
Middle Stage (from class VI—VIII)	1987	95,940	19,910	14,000
Secondary stage (from class IX to X)	1987	42,710	8,360	5,560
Higher secondary stage (from class XI to XII)	,,	18,460	2,360	2,030
Degree College (General)	,,	7,849	229	672
Engineering College	,,	416	58	60
Post Graduate (General)	,,	151	5	14

for educating the tribal people. From the 1957-58 Annual Report it appears that one 'Ashram' type of institution was founded by the Education Directorate at Champaknagar near Agartala for the tribal people alone. The Christian Mission has not also established any separate institution based on purely tribal culture for the said purpose, though it has established a network of other welfare centres with the main purpose of proselytising the tribal peoples. Most surprisingly even now no survey work in low literacy areas is being conducted by the Government. Thus, it is clear that excepting a microscopic number of literate persons receiving a little formal education, the overwhelming majority of the tribal peoples are still non-literate. Accordingly, it can be said that little progress has been made since independence in respect of the spread of education amongst the tribal people of the State. This would be evident from the following Table 5.3.[30]

The Table 5.3 shows that during the year 1987 over the whole State of Tripura only 1,05,700 tribal students attended primary level of education i.e. from class I to class V. In the middle stage the number fell to the tune of 95,940 whereas the number of tribal students is 19,910 only. In the higher secondary stage and particularly in the higher education stage i.e. in the degree and post-graduate classes the number of tribal students is only microscopic in relation to the total number of students of other community. It is also to be noted that most of the tribal boys have neither the means nor any opportunity to receive any formal education even upto the school standard. It is true that some primary schools have no doubt been established in the tribal areas, but these institutions are hardly popular enough to attract the tribal boys and girls. It is really unfortunate that little progress has been made during all these years in respect of the spread of education amongst the tribal people of the State

Employment Services

Regarding employment services amongst the tribes of Tripura, it may be noted that the Central Government made a specific provision for the reservation of posts for the Scheduled Tribes and the percentage of the vacant posts to be reserved for the tribal peoples has been fixed. It is only in 1976-77 that the percentage of the reservation of posts was increased to 29 per cent of the vacant posts of the Central and State Governments.[31] Unfortunately, the State Government had not been strictly following the rules of reservation issued by Central Government. This has been clearly stated in the Annual Report of 1954-55.[32] The following table 5.4 as compiled from the Commissioner's Reports furnishes some important facts relating to registration of names of persons for employment, persons appointed, number of applications submitted directly to the employers, applicants still unemployed, persons employed in the Central and State Governments and in other offices.[33]

TABLE 5.4

State of Tribal Peoples Employment is Services

Years	No. of S.T. applicants	No. of S.T. applicants placed in employment	No. of S.T. applicants submitted to employers	No. of vacancies notified for S.T. applicants only		
				Centre	State	Others
1974-75	934	53	3,177	11	65	6
1975-76-77	—	—	—	—	—	—
1977-78	952	147	—	—	—	—
1978-79	1119	110	—	—	—	—
1979-80	—	—	—	—	—	—

A study of the figures obtained from the above table reveals that the tribal people did not perhaps care to register their names for any appointment. In 1974-75 number of Scheduled Tribe applicants registered was 934 but the number of applicants placed in employment was only 53 while the number of applicants remaining on live register was 3,843. Strangely enough, no report was available during the years 1975-76 and 1977-78. Three years after 1974-75 it was reported that the number of Scheduled Tribe applicants registered remained almost same although the number of applicants placed in employment increased almost thrice. In 1978-79 the figure related to the number of applicants registered increased to the tune of 1,119 but the number of applicants placed in employment was decreased from 147 to 110. Again, in 1970-80 no report was available from the State. If a percentage is taken it would appear that only a very few persons, the percentage being 0.4 per cent, applied for registration of their names. This shows that the tribal people throughout all these years have shown little keenness for employment and accordingly they did not care also to register their names. If we take into consideration the number of persons actually employed out of the registered applicants, the picture is again most unsatisfactory in the sense that out of a large number of registered applicants only a few persons got employment and the total percentage would vary from 10 per cent to 15 per cent of the registered applicants. In the Report of 1978-79, the number of tribals employed in different categories of Central and State Government services has been recorded. It has been reported that out of 288 Class-I posts, the percentage of the tribals is only 2.4 per cent. In the case of 1, 569 Class-II posts, the percentage comes to 4.:3 per cent. Again out of the total number of 2812 Class-III posts and 1323 Class-IV posts, the percentages of tribal persons employed come to 19.66 per cent and 14.9 per cent. Thus it follows that the tribals employed in Central and State Government services are absolutely negligible. The percentage of the total number of persons employed in Government services comes to about 10.03 per cent.[34] The total percentage of the tribal population in the State is 28.45 (1981 Census Report) and the percentage of the employees comes to about 0.2 per cent. This show that the tribal people of Tripura in all these years have not received their due share in employment. It is also surprising that the percentage of tribals in class-IV posts (14.9 per cent) is less than the percentage ef tribals recruited to class III (19.6 per cent).

Again, the occupational classification of tribal population in Tripura as per 1981 Census reveals that total number of main workers amongst them is 2.11 lakhs which is about 36.14 per cent of the total tribal population of 5.84 lakhs.[35] The break up of the main workers, marginal workers and non-workers is given in Table 5.5.[36]

TABLE 5.5
Tribal Workers

Category	No. of persons	Percentage to total tribal population
(A) Main Workers		
(i) Cultivators	1,35,151	23.14
(ii) Agricultural labourers	60,616	10.38
(iii) Household industries etc.	506	0.09
(iv) Other workers	14,786	2.5
(B) Marginal workers	29,813	5.11
(C) Non-workers	3,43,049	58.75

It is thus evident from the above table 5.5 that according to 1981 Cenus Report the main workers constitute 36.14 per cent of the tribal population whereas the number of marginal workers and non-workers constitute 63.86 per cent. This is, even according to Government Report sufficient to indicate the poor economic situation of tribal communities in the State. The same also applies to agricultural labourers and persons engaged in household industries among the tribals in spite of the fact that there are rich resources of forests around their habitats.

Thus, from the occupational classification analysis it is clear that main workers among the tribal communities constitute less than 40 per cent of total tribal population. Moreover, the State Government also had not been strictly following the rules of reservation of posts for Scheduled Tribes. It appears also that most of the reserved vacancies might have been accordingly treated as general for obtaining suitable candidates for the posts. The primary reasons for the non-availability of suitable tribal candidates fulfilling the minimum educational standard required for such jobs lies in their educational drawbacks or absolute lack of education. It implies that illiteracy or lack of formal education may be largely responsible for such a negligible percentage of employed persons in various categories of service. Further, it may be said that most jobs are urban oriented, and the tribal people are very much reluctant to seek jobs in urban areas, the ecological and cultural set up of which is repugnant to the tribals as a whole.

It is quite well known that the tribal peoples of the State mostly dwell in their traditional huts or houses built with all available perishable materials.

Village Housing

In general, the tribal peoples are too poor even to build such huts or houses for their shelters. Naturally, so, they very often take resort to hovel types of shelters which are quite unsuitable for any human habitation. Accordingly, the Central and the State Governments have undertaken financial aid programme for giving financial assistance to the tribal peoples for building their houses in their respective village of localities. Such financial assistances are mostly needed in the case of the resettlement of the Jhumias in the plains for undertaking plough cultivation. Alongwith this granting of financial assistance is associated with the question of rendering medical facilities to the rural tribals. In the Commissioner's Reports, there are certain figures relating to the allocation of funds and expenditure on both these accounts. These would be evident from the following table 5.6.[37]

The table 5.6 contains the allocation of funds for the purpose of housing and medical facilities to be extended to the tribal peoples. From 1969-70 to 1974-75, the fund allocated varied from Rs. 0.20 lakhs to Rs. 2.124 lakhs. It was only from 1977-78 that the amount of fund allocation was raised and in 1978-79 it was Rs. 19.06 lakhs. Regarding the amount spent out of this allocation, it appears that from 1969-70 to 1974-75, an amount less than the allocated one was spent. In 1967-70 a sum Rs. 2.18 lakhs was spent. For all other years, the figures for the amount spent are not available. Then again, during 1975-77 there was no allocation of fund, but the amount spent has been recorded as 0.847 and 0.256. The recurring expenditure for the project considerably increased

TABLE 5.6

Village Housing

Year	Amount sanctioned (in lakhs) Rs.	Amount spent (in lakhs) Rs.
1969-70	* 2.75	2.18
1970-71	—	—
1971-72	0.20	—
1972-73	0.30	—
1973-74	0.45	—
1974-75	2.124	—
1975-76	—	0.847
1976-77	—	0.256
1977-78	2.900	2.900
1978-79	** 19.06	—

* Figure includes both health and housing.

** The amount sanctioned as per Tribal Sub-Plan area.

from 1977-78. The amount sanctioned during the year was Rs. 2.900 lakhs and the amount spent was also the same.

However, it is significant to note that recently there "Rural House Schemes" viz., Low Income Group Housing Schemes, Rural House Sites-cum-Construction Assistance and Housing for the Economically Weaker Section of the Society are being implemented by the State Government and as a result about 2,842 persons are benefitted during the period from 1984-86. Details of the schemes will be evident from the following table 5.7.[38]

TABLE 5.7

Rural Housing Schemes

Year	Low Income Group Housing		Rural House sites-cum-construction		Housing for the economically weaker section	
	Expd. incurred. (Rs. in lakhs)	No. of persons assisted	Expd. incurred (Rs. in (lakhs)	No. of persons assisted	Expd. incurred (Rs. in lakhs)	No. of perons assisted
1984-85	0.87	6	8.93	1191	—	—
1985-86	0.87	6	12.00	1599	6.00	40

From the table 5.7 it appears that no amount of money was sanctioned for the economically weaker section scheme during the year 1984-85. In the same year expenditure incurred for the low income group was only 0.87 lakhs and the number of assisted persons for the whole year was six and strangely enough in the following year that is in 1985-86 expenditure incurred neither increased or decreased and the number of persons benefited remained the same. Of course, the picture of the scheme relating Rural House-Sites-cum Construction is a bit encouraging compared to Low Income Group or the Economically Weaker Section Scheme. It seems that expenditure incurred for the above scheme was Rs. 8.93 lakhs in 1984-85 and in the following year the amount was increased to the tune Rs. 12.00 lakhs and the number of persons assisted was 2,790 for the period from 1984-85 to 1985-86. It is also astonishing to note that although there is provision for special Central assistance in order to cross the poverty line by the Scheduled Tribes, no amount of money was sanctioned for Housing Schemes during the year 1986-87 from that end.[39]

It would appear from the available data as contained in the above tables that little work was done for giving financial assistance to the tribal peoples for building houses and also for extending medical benefits to them. Whatever amount was spent was also most unsatisfactory in regard to their needs. In accordance with the needs of the tribal people, practically speaking, the tribals of Tripura are absolutely bereft of any medical benefits. The Government hospitals or health units are mostly located in urban areas to which the tribal peoples have little access and about which they entertain a repugnant attitude. Naturally so, no adequate provision has yet been made for rendering medical services to the rural tribals living in far off places.

Other Welfare Measures

Besides the above reports relation to various measures adopted or implemented by the Central and State Governments as reported and included in the Commissioner's Reports, there are also certain reports regarding other welfare measures undertaken for the social and economic advancement of the tribal people of the State. Such tribal welfare measures are no doubt various in nature and character, but the Commissioner's Reports contain a few insufficient data with regard to only a few items like the resettlement of the 'Jhumias' for permanent agricultural operations, co-operative marketing societies, loan to individual tribals at a minimum rate of interest, digging of wells and tanks for the supply of drinking water, reclamation of waste lands and distribution of the same including the recovered surplus land for permanent agricultural operation etc. The following table compiled from the available data contained in the Commissioner's Reports furnishes allocation of funds under different years and amounts spent for carrying out certain welfare projects.[40]

TABLE 5.8

Welfare Measures

Year	Allocation made Rs.	Expenditure estimated Rs.
1970-71	18,79,900	15,51,000
1971-72	N.A.	30,00,000
1972-73	45,00,000	45,00,000
1973-74	99,50,000	96,88,900
1974-75	62,50,000	19,86,000
1975-76	N.A.	35,91,700
1977-78	37,90,000	37,90,000
1978-79	N.A.	1,65,000

The above table shows that no reports are available for the year 1971-72, 1975-76 and 1978-79. It indicates there was perhaps no allocation of funds.

From the Commissioner's Reports, it also appears that only records of allocation of funds and estimated expenditure are available, but nothing is known as to the details of the Tribal Welfare Programmes undertaken and implemented by the Central and State Governments. Whatever, a little information available under some years, are also most disappointing, and this has been also recorded in the reports. Even as late as 1971-72, the Commissioner reported that no special cell to give any particular attention to the welfare of the Scheduled Tribe has been created as yet.[41]

It is however, significant to note that for the improvement or betterment of the economic condition of the tribal people, it was decided that the allotment of distributive agencies or quotas to the Scheduled Tribes on preferential basis could play an important role. It has been accordingly stressed in the Commissioner's Report that the Government agencies and public sector undertakings should sanction retail dealership to suitable unemployed graduates and other entrepreneurs belonging to the Scheduled Castes and Scheduled Tribes Communities. The Commissioner made an attempt to collect information from the State Governments concerned in this regard, but most regrettably no information could be supplied during the period from 1977-78 to 1979-80. It has been recorded in the Commissioner's Report that only in 1978-79, eighty-eight such Agencies were distributed. It is thus clear that even in this particular field the State Government did not carry out the directive of the Commissioner and nothing have been done so far.

It is also interesting to note that the Government of India issued instruction in the month of August, 1974 to the State Government that the Integrated Tribal Development Project (ITDP) have to be prepared keeping in view the problems of specific areas by the end of 1975-76 and the State Government spent Rs. 0.82 lakhs in 1976-77 for preparation of such a report on the ITDP for North Tripura District only through Agricultural Finance Corporation, Bombay. Surprisingly enough, the project report which was received in 1976-77 had not been implemented till 1982. While a similar project for South Tripura District was prepared departmentally in 1980, the project was not implemented.[42]

The State Government's own documents admit that the Scheduled Tribes have remained much of the time outside the development process. According to Government Report of 1980, "The benefits of modern education, communication and health care have remained concentrated in the Western segment of the State leaving out large areas in eastern parts largely inhabited by Scheduled Tribes far behind in respect of various amenities."[43]

Thus, the overall picture of the Central and State Government undertakings in respect of safeguarding the interest of the tribal peoples for which the Constitutional provisions have been made is also dismal. Consequently, the socio-economic condition of the tribal peoples of Tripura has undergone little changes. No remarkable progress or advancement regarding any aspect of their life is noticeable. Most of the tribals are still living in abject poverty. But at the same time marked transformation of their life-patterns have taken place. There has been no economic improvement of advancement, but their outlook has changed considerably due to close contact with the outsiders. Their cultural patterns have been transformed, but there has been little progress in their economic upliftment. This created an anomalous situation in the tribal society of Tripura. Because of the cultural transformation the tribal peoples have learnt and adopted many things, and at the same time they have become more and more conscious about their own rights and priviliges. They are all discontended and frustrated peoples because of various forms of exploitation carried out for a long time past. Naturally so, discontentment, frustration, anger and hatred against the exploiters kindled in the hearts of the tribals so long could no more be kept suppressed, and its manifestations in all kinds of organised or unorganised movements or uprisings highlighting their grievances began spreading like wild fire, even conflagrating the whole State of Tripura. This is evident from the tribal discontents and uprisings that have taken place in the State of Tripura from time to time.

REFERENCES

1. Roy Burman, B.K. : *Demographic and Socio-economic Profiles of the Hill Areas of North-East India*, Ministry of Home Affairs, New Delhi, 1970.
2. Sarin, V.I.K. : *India's North-East in Flames*, New Delhi, 1980, p. 94.

3. *Ibid.*
4. *Ibid.*
5. *Ibid.*
6. *Ibid* p. 95
7. *Ibid.*
8. *Ibid.*
9. *Bengal Judicial Proceedings* : March, 1861 Nos. 16.
10. Mackenzie, Sir Alexander : *Memorandum on the North-East Frontier of Bengal,* Calcutta, 1869, p. 67.
11. Buckland, C.E. : *Bengal under the Lieutenant Governors,* Vol. I, Calcutta,1901, p. 181-2.
12. *Report of the Commissioner for the Scheduled Castes and Scheduled Tribes.*
13. *Ibid.*
14. *Three years of work 1982-85* : *Tripura Tribal Autonomous District Council,* Agartala, p. 12
15. *Ibid.*
16. *Memorandum submitted to the Eighth Finance Commission by Tripura Tribal Areas Autonomous District Council,* Agartala, p. 1.
17. *Ibid.*
18. Roy, Jagatjyoti : *Bidroha Bibartan-O-Tripura,* Agartala, 1985, p. 74
19. *Frontline,* June 21-July 10, 1987.
20. *Three years of Work 1982-85 TAADC,* Agartala, p. 12
21. *Report on Development of Tribal Areas,* New Delhi, 1981, p. 30.
22. *Report af the Commissioner of Scheduled Castes and Scheduled Tribes,* 1953-54.
23. *Ibid.*
24. Tripura Government Tribal Welfare Department.
25. Menon, K.D. : *Tripura District Gazetteers* 1975.
26. *Ibid.*
27. *Ibid.*
28. *Draft Annual Sub-Plan* (Government of Tripura), 1987-88.
29. Menon, K.D. : *Tripura District Gazetteers,* 1975.
30. *Statistical and Review Section,* Education Department, Agartala, 1987.
31. *Report of the Commissioner, S.C. & S.T.,* 1953-54 p. 57.
32. *Ibid*
33. *Ibid.*
34. *Ibid.*

35. *Tribal Sub-Plan for Annual Plan,* 1986-87.
36. *Ibid.*
37. *Report of the Commissioner, S.C. & S.T.*
38. *Tribal Sub-Plan for Annual Plan,* 1986-87.
39. *Ibid.*
40. *Report of the Commissioner, S.C. & S.T.,* 1971-72.
41. *Ibid.*
42. *Audit Report on the Integrated Tribal Development Project,* 1982.
43. *Report of the Dinesh Singh Committee,* August, 1980, p. 27 (Manuscript).

SIX

TRIBAL UPRISINGS (1767—1980)

The Tribal Communities of Tripura have been consistently deprived of their lands and forests and other sources of subsistence even when Tripura was under the rule of *Maharajas*. These deprivals of basic necessities of their very existence moved them to disregard, and even to armed-revolt. Sometimes, these were fostered by the family strifes over the throne. Contesting claimants also tried to occupy power with the help of some disconted tribes. It is, however, possible to discern two distinct phases of tribal insurgency in Tripura. The first phase lasted from 1767 to 1946, while the period from 1947 formed the second phase.

First Phase

The earliest account of insurrection in Tripura may be dated back to the sixth decade of the 18th Century when Samser Gazi, a revenue clerk revolted against Nasir Mahammed, Zaminder of Dakshinik Pargana. Samser organised a band of soldiers by training-up poor peasants. It has been reported that Mog Community of Tripura also joined Samser in his campaign against the Zamindar of Chakla Roshnabad.[1] It may be noted in this context that the territorial pattern of Tripura, at that time was divided into two parts viz., the hilly area and the plains. In the hill, the ruler was independent but in the plains, known as 'Chakla Roshnabad', he was a Zamindar under the Nawabs of Bengal. It is interesting to note that this peculiar arrangement was prevalent even during the Mughal period. Steward wrote, "The province of Tippera, which from times immemorial had been independent' Kingdom became annexed to the Mughal empire, after the Mughal invasion of Tripura. The situation as it prevailed in 'Tippera' during the Mughal period formed a legacy for the Britishers. Acting upon the Mughal arrangements, the British rulers attached to the British territory only the plain portion of 'Tippera, known as 'Chakla Roshnabad' and confirmed therein only the Zamindari right of the King of Tippera".[2] Thus, the hills became 'Independent Tippera' and the King was an ordinary Zamindar on the plains, reigns as independent prince over 3,000 sq. miles of upland, and was for many years a more absolute monarch than Scindia or Patliala..."[3]

The Maharaja of Tripura was always interested in the Zamindari of Chakla Roshnabad because this was the only paying part of Tripura whereas, the hill area was barren, covered with jungles inhabited by tribals who commonly practised *Jhuming*, the practice of which was not conducive to the emergence of a political entity.[4] Naturally, the ruler of Tripura had to depend on the Chakla Roshnabad for larger revenue. Reference may be made in this context that since the acquisition of *Dewani* of Chakla Roshnabad in 1761, East India Company increased the rate of rent payable by the Zamindar to the tune of Rs. 66,695 and within four years i.e., in 1765 the amount was again increased to Rs. 1,05,000.[5] This was no doubt a heavy burden on the shoulder of a Zamindar but in a traditional manner he not only shiftèd the tax but out of covetousness tried to exact as much revenue as possible from the peasants. This accounted for intolerable poverty of the peasants. They were also subjected to cruel exactions. Many peasants lost their lands because of their inability to pay rent in time. Unfortunately, many of them were converted into slaves by the landholders. Samser Gazi himself was a slave. He saw the poverty of the peasants and cruel exaction of revenue by the Zamindar. Circumstances thus led him to be rebel against the oppressive Zamindar. With the help of some poor peasants and tribals he revolted against his master. The people of the Mog community joined him in the above revolt because they wanted to liberate themselves from the subjugation and oppression of Tripura Kings.

Maharaja Indra Manikya ruler of Tripura sent a force to suppress seditious Samser but the royal force was defeated and the ruler of Tripura was forced to recognise him as Zamindar of Dashinik.[6] Gradually, Samser became the ruler of Chakla Roshnabad. He also defeated Krishna Manikya, brother of Indra Manikya and occupied Udaipur. He assumed the title Shri Shrijut Mohammed Samser Choudhury Zamindar.[7] "Samser was a benevolent ruler". This is evident from record maintained by Sinha (1896) who wrote : "Samser built several forts, fixed the prices of essential commodities and introduced a system of standard weight in the market."[8] Not only that, he distributed lands to the landless slaves and peasents.[9] But in spite of his magnanimous activities for the commoners, he was dethroned. It was because the royalists appealed to the Nawab of Bengal alleging that Samser was as an oppressive ruler and a dacoit. According to Noakhali District Gazetteer, Samser extorted one lakh of rupees from a miserly Zamindar who did not spend money for the welfare of his subjects.[10] The Governor of Chittagong was not happy with Samser. He was made captive and was shot dead at the mouth of a canon at Rangpur Ghoranghat.[11] This was an opportune moment for Krishna Manikya. He immediately recovered the throne and was recognised as the ruler of Tripura by the Nawab.[12]

From the above account, it would not be unjustified to conclude that the root of the revolt lay in the acute economic crisis and unbearable poverty of the people. Moreover, boundless covetousness and the method of cruel exaction of revenue and above all, misrule and injustice on the part of Zamindar moved the commoners to armed revolt.

The next tribal uprisings took place in 1857 when Sepoy Mutiny gave a shooting pain to the British Raj. It was at that time British imperialism introduced "Doctrine of Lapse" and "Subsidiary Alliance." Both the systems guaranted the native Princes in the possession of their dominions under British protection. It may be noted that formerly native rulers who were weak or oppressive were generally overthrown by a quiet revolution in the Palace but the new arrangements under the Doctrine of Lapse of Lord Dalhousie were effective guarantee for the security of every protected Prince and that such native ruler was no longer exposed to the danger of loss of his thrown. Naturally, Ishan Chandra Manikya (1850-62) was very eager to appease the British rulers in the interest of the security of his Kingdom. Naturally, when the Sepoys of the 34th Native Infantry mutinied at the Chittagong on the night of 18th November, 1857, plundered the treasury and then marched to Agartala for shelter, Ishan Chandra Manikya sent Tripura army to drive the mutineers out from his Kingdom. In support of this statement reference may be made of W. Hunter who observes in his *Statistical Account of Bengal*, that the small infantry force at the Raja's disposal did not enable him to oppose the whole body of Sepoys.[7] He, however, issued orders to arrest and delivery to the British authorities of all mutineers found wandering within the limits of Hill Tipperah.[13]

Besides, King Ishan Chandra had to bear the burden of his father's debts which estimated about eleven lakhs rupees. Now, to solve this financial problem, Ishan Chandra Manikya appointed Balaram Hazari as his *dewan* and entrusted him the sole management of his Kingdom. Balaram and his brother Sridam exploited the situation by cruel exaction of revenue.[14] As a result, people of the Tripuri Community under their two leaders Kirti and Parikshit revolted against the King. This revolt in 1857 was the first tribal revolt against the King's oppression in Tripura. The report goes that in the midnight, the rebels attacked the House of Balaram Hazari and killed Sridam. Balaram however, managed to escape. The revolt was ultimately suppressed by army. Many rebels were imprisoned and Kirti was killed through a conspiracy.[15]

Within the span of three years, since Tripra Revolt of 1857, there took place a series of raids by the Kuki tribe in

Tripura. These raids were commonly known as the "Great Kuki invasion of 1860". According to Mackenzie (1869), in the early part of 1860, a large body of Kukis after raiding the Upper Feni burst into the plains of Tipperah at Chagulneyah, burnt or plundered 15 villages, butchered 185 British subjects and carried off about 101 captives.[16] Not only that, the Kukis took away from these villages gold, silver and iron. The Maharaja of Tripura sent troops immediately to the spot but the Kukis already retired to jungle.[17] It was believed that raiders were the followers of Ruttan Poiyas whose clan was known to live far up between the sources of the Feni and Karanphuli river.[18] The British authority was, however, unhappy with the ruler of Tripura for His Majesty's inability to prevent the raiders from entering into the British territory. The King was forced to pay Rs. 6,850 as compensation. Later on, in January, 1861, the British authority sent Captain Raban to punish the rebel Kukis. Captain Raban straight way went to Ruttan Poiyas village but in the meantime the Kukis fled into the jungles by setting fire to the approach to the Kuki Villages. The English force destroyed about 15 hundred mounds of paddy of Kukis. While the rebel Kukis in collaboration with the Reangs made a fierce attack on Udaipur, the old Capital of Tripura. As a result, about 150 persons were killed, 200 were carried away as captives and large destruction of property was made.[19] The raiders, however, were beaten off from Kurkuria Police Post and suffered a considerable loss from a bold attack made upon them by Military Police commanded by an Indian Officer.[20] Historical record shows that the movement was directed by certain near relatives of the Tripura Raja. Mackenzie says, "the main instigators of the invasion were three or four Hill Tipperah refugees, Thakurs who had lived sometime among the Kukis and who took advantage of the ill-feeling caused by an attack made by the Raja's subjects. Driven by the Raja from his dominions, these men had formed alliances among the various Kuki tribes of the interior and year by year villages supposed to be friendly to the Raja, had been attacked and plundered. Some of the Raja's own subjects, moreover exasperated by his constant exactions were believed to have invited the Kukis to ravage his territories.[21]

The fundamental fact, however, remains that during the later years of the reign of King Ishan Chandra Manikya, Tripura was in a turmoil. The King did not nominate the Jubaraj or heir apparent for the throne. This caused palace intrigues of the various candidates for the throne. Besides, the King disbanded his army and totally neglected his police. As a result, the King failed to restore law and order in the State. Again, the King empowered his Guru Bipin Behari Goswami, a Bengali Brahmin to conduct every State matter. In fact, he was responsible for the misrule of the administration. Many of the people in the hills suffered by the inhuman extortions. Their rents had been enormously enhanced and they were at all time liable to oppressiou of somekind. Mention may be made that the then Magistrate of Tipperah in his account of the administration of the Maharaja reported in 1863 that rents were collected at the point of Bayonet.[22] As regards Reang's participation in the Kuki movement, it may be pointed out that the Reangs were suffering from acute economic hardship. They were forced to borrow money from the Mahajans of Khandal Pargana at a very high rate of interest. Such economic condition as recorded in K.C. Sinha's Rajmala quoted in N.R. Roychoudhury's Tripura through the ages'. The report goes that there was no rains for two or three years in the hills. They could not cultivate land. There was scarcity or no food in their homes. They were at the point of starvation but debt did not remain static rather increased at a galloping rate. The Mahajans began to harass these Reangs for money. Naturally, to free themselves from the clutches of cruel Mahajans, the Reangs joined the Kukis.[23]

It is thus evident from the above account that the tribal movements of 1857 and 1860 were, in fact, tribal uprisings against oppression and injustice of the feudal authority.

Again, another revolt known as 'Jamatia Revolt' took place in 1863 under their leader Parikshit. For a proper analysis of the nature and origin of the revolt, it is necessary to focus light on the socio-economic and geo-political conditions of Tripura. Hunter says, 'In the hills there are no tenures at all, the system of agriculture, that is, Jhuming adopted by the hill tribes preventing them from cultivating same plot of land for two years in succession...no rent is paid for land used for Jhuming ; but in lieu of rent a tax is levied upon each family, the hill-people being assessed according to their tribes." It may also be noted that during the financial year 1874-75 Reangs were supposed to pay House tax at the rate of Rs. 10.00 whereas the Tripuris, the Jamatias were required to pay Rs. 3.50 but Halam's share was fixed at Rs. 2.00 only.[24] Thus, clear discrimination or injustice in the system of taxation was prevalent in the tribal society. Moreover, the collection of tax gave every opportunity for exactions even to the lowest official concerned. Surprisingly enough, not only does the actual collector exacts his share and have himself and his followers conveyed free of expense from village to village but the whole party required to be fed and a percentage is levied by the peons. The fees paid under various pretences are said to amount frequently to 50 per cent on the tax as originally settled ; nor does the Raja profit by these extra cesses, except in so far that he can thereby afford to underplay his subordinates.[25]

On the otherside, political situation was also chaotic and uncertain. While Birchandra Manikya succeeded his brother Ishan Chandra Manikya in 1862, his succession to the throne was challenged by half brothers Nilkrishna and Kalathakur who brought a suit in the court claiming that Birchandra was never apointed *Jubraj* or heir apparent to the throne by his brother Ishan Chandra. Nabadwip Chandra, who was the only surviving legitimate son of Ishan Chandra Manikya also made a suit against Birchandra Manikya. As a result, the dispute about the succession to the throne remained unsettled and people apprehended that they may be required to pay revenue twice or thr ce because there were two or more claimants to the throne. So, people were not willing to pay their rents at such risks. It is in this socio-economic and political background, King Birchandra sent Dakhrai Hazari, an officer to collect rent from the subjects. The fact that Mr. Hazari tried to extract from them some undue privileges specially forced *Coolie*-labour. The Jamatias protested against forced Coolie labour. It may be noted in this context, that in the absence of internal roads and communications at that time, movement in the hills was very difficult. To meet this difficulty, the 'Taitun' system or forced Coolie labour was introduced. Under this system when the king or his officials moved into the hills, the hill people had to provide them with guides and labour for carrying the goods upto the next village. The later villages would follow the former ones by rotation. This way the goods were relayed to the destination.[26] Now, the Jamatias not only protested against this taitun system but also refused to pay rent on succession issue. Dakhai Rai being humiliated reported to the King that the Jamatias were preparing for a revolt. Unfortunately, the King without making any enquiry sent army to collect rent from the Jamatias by force. The outcome of this condition was the Jamatia revolt (1863). The revolt was however suppressed with utmost cruelty by the Kuki soldiers. Such an event is recorded in the Bengal Judicial Proceedings, October, 1864 No. 47 quoted in N. Roy Choudhury's *Tripura Through the Ages* (1977) which states, "about 200 Tipperahs (Jamatias) have been killed, many villages burnt down, the inhabitants of which are wandering about the plains of Tipperah". In support of this document Sinha (1890) observes, "Two hundred heads of Jamatias were brought to Agartala by the Kukis, as a token of their victory."[27] Finally, Parikshit, the leader of the Jamatias was captured and brought to the King. The King however, released him later on after converting the Jamatias to Vaishnavism.[28]

After Jamatia revolt, (1863) there were no examples of such occurrences of tribal insurgency till 1942. But the rulers of Tripura realised that meagre income based on Jhuming only is just insufficient to run a State machinary. It is, therefore, to augment the revenue of the State, the rulers of Tripura invited the Bengalis to settle there practising wet rice cultivation, processing of agricultural products, carpentry, blacksmithy etc. Subsequently, such settlements in the plains of Tripura led not only to increased agricultural production but also to the expansion of trade.[30] In fact, both these developments helped to increase revenue collection without which, the Kings could not have built up the administrative and military structure so essential for consolidating power and the ability to rule over the State.[31] Then in the natural process the Maharaja's of Tripura started adopting the Muslim and in the later period British system of administration. Experts are of opinion that from the time of Mahamanikya, that in the early part of 15th Century Tripura entered the era of the State formation process with Muslim pattern of administration. Whereas, the modern period in the history of Tripura dates from the time of Birchandra Manikya who reorganised the executive and judicial administration after the British India fashion. As a result, the whole administrative machinery was controlled, manned and managed by the advanced peoples. They were employed in the royal services and enjoyed all sorts of privileges and patronage from the Court. These advanced people were all Bengalees who migrated to Tripura in search of more economic gains or profits. The settlement of the Bengalees under the royal patronage proved disastrous to the subsistence economy of the tribal communities of Tripura. The Maharaja of Tripura, however, was guided by the fundamental objective of furthering improvement of advancement of States' economy and cultural entrepot or rather to modernise them. The motivation of such settlement of land will be clear from the following excerpt taken from the "proceedings of the *Shahshan Sanmilani* of 1323 T.E. (1913 A.D.) : "...the system of permanent settlement should be continued. Instead of distributing small pieces of land, large areas of 500 *drons* (3200 acres) or more in one block should be given out in permanent settlement. This measure will lead to an increase in the number of rich and cultured persons as also of ordinary tenants. And if, rich wealthy and resourceful persons take such *taluka* (estates) then by their endeavour, roads and other means of communication will be built up which will open-out the way for general development and prosperity of the State."[32]

Such alluring offer was a big incentive for the non-tribals of the neighbouring districts of Bangladesh such as Comilla, Noakhali, Sylhet, Mymonsingh etc. and as a result the State also received a continuous flow of immigrant land hungry population.

The King perhaps could not realise that such settlement of the Bengalees on a large scale and granting of all sorts of privileges would fall so heavily on the interests and welfare of the tribal communities of his state. Being subjected to persistent exploitation, the tribal peoples also started realising that their economic interests were being seriously hampered by the settlement of the Bengalees from the plains and outside. This created a feeling of discontent and distrust between the two broadly divided communities of Tripura, viz., the tribal and non-tribal, the latter again being mostly the Bengali Hindus. Besides, there was the third faction supplied by the Christian Missionaries. It may be noted in this context that from the first half of the twentieth century Christian Missionary activities began in Tripura with the primary object of proselytising the tribal peoples under the garb of emancipating them from their socio-economic bondage. At that time two Christian Missionaries were established. One at Mariamnagar in 1930 and the other at Arundhatinagar in 1937. These Christian Missionaries established churches and began all sorts of welfare activities in the tribal areas by opening schools and establishing hospitals, asylums, orphanges, shelter-houses, etc. All these welfare activities were being continued with the object of ameliorating the sufferings and miseries of the tribal peoples and also to elevating them from their socio-economic bondage. It has been a policy with the Christian Mission to win the confidence of the tribal people through these welfare activities and to a great extent, they have succeeded amongst some tribes of Tripura. This will be evident from the fact that during 1901, 1921 and 1941 Census the entire population of Kuki tribe returned themselves as Hindus but during 1961 Census 42.40 per cent returned themselves as Christians, 57.58 per cent as Hindus and 0.02 per cent did not state their religion.[33] Again, in case of the Lushai Community during 1901 Census the entire population returned themselves as Christians and 2.23 per cent as Hindus. Whereas in 1961 Census 98.73 per cent have returned themselves as Christian, 0.74 per cent as Hindus and 0.53 per cent as Buddhists.[34]

Thus, Christianity achieved great success in proselytising some major tribes like Garos, Lushais and Kukis who mostly live in isolated regions. Amongst some other tribes also the Christianity has been able to make some headway. And as a result of the activities of the Christian missions some of the tribals have become a little educated and the Missionaries have succeeded in making them more and more conscious about the large scale exploitations carried out mostly by the Bengali Hindus and thereby the Christian Mission succeeded in creating a feeling of estrangement between the tribal and non-tribal population of the State.

Discontents amongst the tribal people and their grievances against the non-tribals, more particularly in respect of grabing the tribal land, became very acute in the third decade of the present Century when Maharaja Bir Bikram (1923-1947) could realise the situation to the extent that if the tribal land-grabing by the non-tribals continued unabated, the tribal communities in the State would be deprived of their subsistence economy and their very existence would be jeopardised. Accordingly, for the first time, the *Maharaja* wanted to put a stop to this continuous process of the land-grabing by the non-tribals. That is why, the Maharaja by an order in 1340 T.E. (1930-31 A.D.) reserved a wide area of 11,000 *drones* (28.490 hectares) in the Khowai sub-divisions for five tribes viz., *Tipras, Jamatias Reangs, Noatias* and *Halams.* Subsequenty, the total scheduled reserved tribal areas was raised to 5,05,053 hectares in 1941.[35] It may be noted here that this reservation was, however, made only for five tribes and others were excluded. Not only that, this reservation was restricted only to one sub-division. Naturally this reservation of tribal land could not satisfy all the tribal communities of Tripura, and the land grabing by the non-tribals continued unabated in other parts of the State.

Realising the prevailing discontent amongst the people some community and progressive minded youths of Tripura formed a popular organisation under the title "Tripura Rajya Jana Mangal Samity" in 1937 and a few months later another organisation viz., "Tripura Rajya Ganaparishad" was formed by some Congress minded youths. Both these organisations were active at that time organising movements in support of popular demands. It is to be noted in this context that the Communist party was put under a legal ban in 1934 which lasted till mid 1942. However, its activities continued in a different fashion. As for instance, the Congress Socialist Party which was set up in 1934-35 included a number of Communists. In fact, before its legalization in July 1942, the Communist party workers worked under different organisations throughout the country. In Tripura, the Communists worked under the banner 'Janamangal Samity'. The organisation raised the slogan of responsible Government under the aegis of the Maharaja along with its ten-point political and sixteen point social and economic demand.[36] Tripura Rajya Ganaparishad also on the other hand, raised the demand for responsible Government side by side with its twenty-point charter of demands including those for abolition of *Taitung* (a system by which villagers were compelled to carry luggage etc. of the official on tour), some feudal taxes viz., *Ghar-Chukti* (family tax), *Ghasuri* (tax on cutting of grass), removal of all restrictions on political activities and introduction of land reforms etc. formed the spearhead of this movement. The peasants were organised under the slogan of 'land for tillers' and the demand for giving lands to the tribal Jhumias (practising shifting cultivation) and landless agriculturist were focussed before public eye with increasing force.[37]

Thus, the movements launched by *Janamangal Samity Tripura Rajya Ganaparished* with their demands became very wide spread all over Tripura and these movements to a limited extent were accompanied by violent expression as well. Such movements were, however, not typical to the native State of Tripura, rather these were more or less common to other native States of India. The then Tripura administration thought that if they could guide the political consciousness of the people under likewise organisation viz., Janamangal Samity on the Constitutional channel with moderate demands, it could then save Tripura from many troubles as some of the native States of India were confronted with. It is evident from police reports that with the above motives, two publicity officers of the *Maharaja*, silently joined the Janamangal.[38] The aim was to channelise the movement in a Constitutional manner and thereby making it congenial to the princely State. But the hopes of the State machinery were belied. The Samity became very popular among the masses through numerous public meetings and pamphlets. Finally, the intensity of the movement was so pressing that the Maharaja had to pass the Praja Mandal Act in 1938. This Act included provisions for the election of the members of the *Praja Mandal* on communal basis i.e., Bengali Hindus, Muslims and the Tripura *Kshatriyas* that is the tribals. It may be noted that Maharaja might have included this provision of election on communal basis after the Government of India Act of 1935. Even this did not satisfy either the *Jānamangal Samity* or the Tripura Rajya Gana Parishad and violent expressions of their dissatisfaction continued, but things changed to a worse situation with the break-out of the Second World War. In order to suppress popular movement many top ranking leaders like Bansi Thakur (Amarendra Deb Burman), Prabhat Roy, Biren Dutta, Nimai Deb Burman were held in detention as security prisoners and subsequently sent to Jails under D.I. Rules.[39] Not only that, since, the beginning of the year 1940, all meetings and processions were banned and thus civil liberty was totally curbed. The security prisoners are reported to have been treated very badly but this report was subsequently denied by the Maharaja of Tripura.[40] It has also been reported that during the year 1939 a deputation was sent from Tripura to Gandhiji who was then at Malikanda in the Dacca District. He was reported to have advised them to put up a relentless fight against feudal oppressions with courage and determination.[41] It is also reported that even a section of the Maharaja's armed force became restive in the face of political storm.[42]

The situation became very tense and it took little time even for a Scheduled Tribe to rise against the existing feudal pattern of society which was oppressive in nature. The movement was launched by one Ratanmani, who hailed from Chittagong Hill Tracts. It may be noted in this context that like all other tribal societies in Tripura, the Reang Society was also dominated by the village headmen who were locally known as *Choudhuries.* The head of these Choudhuries was called Rai. According to tribal social organisation, the commoners always depend upon them i.e., the Choudhuries for any decision of social, economic and political nature. Now, the authority and powers of the *Choudhuries* was enhanced and supported by the policy of the Kings. They collected tax through the *Choudhuries.* Being endowed with the privileged position, the choudhuries did not hesitate to make various exactions from the common people.

The Reangs under the leadership of Ratanmani protested against this oppressive feudal system. Further, the Reangs were highly dissatisfied with the unequal taxation system of the King. The rate of the tax varied according to the tribe to which the family belonged.[43] It has been reported that the Halams and Tripuris paid minimum taxes while the Reangs and Noatias had to pay maximum. In support of this, reference may be made of the statement of Shri Umakanta Das (1903) who already observed that the Reangs were over-taxed.[44] They not only had to give highest House Tax but also Bamboo and Cane Taxes. Naturally so, the Reangs protested against these inequalities but without any effect. They approached Ratanmani and it was under his guidance that the socio-economic movement among the Reangs and Noatias gathered its strength.

In the meantime the Second World War broke out. The Maharaja of Tripura gave his full support and co-operation to the British Government. The entire resources of the State and personal services of the ruler had been placed at the disposal of the British Crown. The Maharaja wanted to raise a band of soldiers from the Reang Community and with this perspective, the Maharaja ordered the Choudhuris to collect soldiers from the Reang Community. But the Choudhuris failed to recruit Reang youths because Ratanmani created resistance against recruitment. It has been also reported that Udaipur, Bagafa, Amarpur, Belonia were against the administration. The Maharaja immediately sent a strong army to crush the rebel Reangs. The rebels finally, however, could not stand against the Royal force. Their villages were burnt and many of them were arrested and brought to Agartala.

Ratanmani and some of his followers fled to Chittagong Hill Tracts but they were arrested by the British Police and put to Rangamati Jail. The Chief Minister of Tripura made a request to the British Political Agent (1943) to issue extradition warrants for the arrest and prosecution of the accused persons.[45] Accordingly, Ratanmani was handed over to Tripura administration. After a few hours he is alleged to have been produced before the Maharaja and he met with unnatural death.[46] No doubt, the Maharaja was successful in crushing the revolt, but the martyr Ratanmani's death opened up a new horizon for tribal movement in Tripura.

Second Phase (1947-80)

When World War was over, the order of ban on political organisations was vacated and subsequently the leaders of both the Janamangal Samity and the Ganaparishad were released from Jail. The people of Tripura became more and more politically conscious and all efforts of the various organisations, tribal and non-tribal were directed towards abolishing monarchy in the State of Tripura. Politically conscious peoples of the State became sharply divided into two rival camps viz., camps consisting of peoples with left leanings and those with right leanings. Thus, Janamangal Samity was dissolved and an organisation named *Tripura Rajya Praja Mandal* was formed by the ex-members of Janamangal Samity who were mostly members of the Communist Party whereas the Tripura State Congress Committee was formed with the members of the Tripura Rajya Ganaparishad. It is important to note that the Maharaja did not recognise the left leanings i.e. the Tripura Rajya Praja Mandal but made an arrangement for a big conference of the tribal communities at Agartala and declared in that conference that he would soon from a responsible Ministry for Tripura. But the leaders of the Praja Mandal publicly opposed the proposal as the members of the proposed Ministry were to be nominated by the king according to his own choice.[47] By this time, the struggle for independence reached a decisive phase and the King of Tripura desired to acceede to the proposed Indian Union before his death in May, 1946. After the death of the King, his son

Kirit Bikram became the Maharaja of Tripura. Since Kirit Bikram was a minor at that time Council of Regency under the Presidentship of Maharani Kanchan Prava Debi, [widow of the dead Maharaja, was formed to run the administration. But within a few months after the death of Maharaja Bir Bikram, Tripura fell to the prey of conspiracy manoeuvred by some leading persons of Comilla of erstwhile East Pakistan. In support of this fact Sardar Patel's correspondence (3rd November, 1947) may be mentioned as point of reference : "The Muslim League National Guards in East Bengal are carrying on open propaganda that Tripura State belongs to Eastern Pakistan and that preparations are being made to invade Tripura". The situation was tense throughout the State.[48] Prime Minister Nehru wrote to Sardar Vallabbhai Patel, "You are no doubt aware of the reports that there is trouble brewing on the borders of Tripura (Agartala) State. It is said that the Muslim National Guards from East Bengal, Tripura District have started an agitation against the accession of Tripura to the Indian Union and they may well have raids. Tripura State is very feeble and the Raj family itself is divided. If any trouble occurs there, we have no means of reaching it except by Assam. Yesterday I sent a telegram to the Pakistan Government warning them about this matter. I have also informed the Assam Government, I hope that you will deal directly with the Tripura State authority. Evidently the present Dewan is not much good and a better and a stronger man is needed. Dr. P.C.Ghosh has also written to me on this subject and drawn urgent attention to it".[49] Government of India, however, spared no time after this note and immediately sent necessary materials to put an end to the inimical inroads and influences. The Council of Regency was dissolved and Maharani Kanchan Prava Debi became sole Regent. The resignation of the Chief Minister S.V.Mukherjee was accepted and a new Chief Minister for the State was appointed on the recommendation of the Government of India. It was also declared the Chief Minister, hereafter be designated as the Dewan of Tripura State who with the assistance of one Adviser and two or three Secretaries will run the administration.[50]

It is at that time the new administration faced another tribal revolt in Golaghati. A section of the tribal community mostly Tiprahs protested against the dishonest merchants, money-lenders and above all against the misrule and injustice of the Government. To realise the poverty and sufferings of the hill people a probe into their financial condition may be relevant. Bijoy Kumar Sen, the then Dewan of the Government of Tripura recorded in the State Gazette Memo No. 2, 1323 T.E. Bhadra 29 that most of the Mahajans were corrupt. They used to tempt the Jhumias by giving them loan at a very high rate of interest. Poor Jhumias were quite ignorant even about simple calculation and as such, they became easy prey at the hands of the dishonest Mahajans who ultimately grabbed not only their product but land itself.[51] Besides, sudden rise of price due to war and post-war conditions (Second World War) and acute food crisis pushed them to starvation condition. An outcome of this condition was the Golaghati Tribal Revolt of 1948. The story goes that on 9th October, 1948, the famine-sticken peasants mostly of Tiprah tribal community detained forcefully a food-grain loaded boat at Golaghati bound for Bishalgarh. The owner of the boat was Mr. Haricharan Saha. To save the situation Mr. Saha assured the starving peasants that he would distribute food-grains among them free of cost in presence of a Government official, but secretly he informed the police about illegal detention of the boat and urged them to disperse the aggrieved peasants. The police opened fire several rounds unwarrantedly on the starving people and instantly killed nine tribals and many others were wounded.[52] The situation became very grave and tense. Tribal peasants became militant and were burning with the fire of revenge. Secretly they formed a number of militant squads with the retired army-men of Tripura.[53] Meanwhile, a big influx of refugees took place due to partition of the country and the process of immigration also remained unabated. The Government started giving them settlements at the cost of the tribals. At this time *Praja Mandal* came to the forefront for the safety and security of the lives and property of the hill people who subsequently started a strong resistance movement. The Government also began to post military camps in different interior areas of the State in order to crush the movement. The hill people were subjected to torture and repression for their alliance with the Praja Mandal. Later on, in order to cope with the situation the tribal leaders dissimulated the banner "Tripura Rajya Parishad" with Dasarath Deb Burma and Aghore Deb Burma as its President and Secretary respectively.[54] The Parishad demanded immediate withdrawl of DIR and grant of freedom of expression and of forming association. But instead of conceding the demands, the authority ruthlessly suppressed the movemet. Majumder (1985) quotes Tripur Chandra Sen in his 'The Struggle for Responsible Governmet in Tripura (1947-1956)' that the support of an All India Party behind the movement was badly felt at this stage and hence, the leaders of Mukti Parishad and Krishak Samity assembled together and formed a branch of the Communist Party in Tripura in 1949. The repression let loose by the administration went on increasing. It was reported that ten tribal villages under Jirania Police Station were burnt. Many houses situated at the Mouzas of Jampuijala, Ghanimar and Sidhai were looted. In Khowai Sub-Division, the villages within the area were burnt and looted. The most brutal of all was the firing at Padmabil where three tribal women were killed.[55] Naturally, in self-defence the people in the hills stood united and formed a militant squad named 'Santi Sena Bahini'. This militant tribal group began to counter the Government forces with their ancestral muzzle loader. The situation, thus became further aggravated. The Government of India then decided to take over the administration of the State without further delay. To quote Sardar Patel, "the reason lay in the inability of the State, at that stage of development to solve a host of problems brought before it by partition".[56] Accordingly, the merger was signed by the Regent Kanchan Prava Debi on behalf of her minor son Prince Kirit Bikram Manikya Bahadur on 9th September, 1949 and the State was taken over as Chief Commissioner's province on 15th October, 1949. Thus formal integration of Tripura with the rest of India was completed but unfortunately no step was taken to solve the problems of the hill people of Tripura.

Now, with the attainment of independence the Praja Mandal was mainly concerned with the struggle for responsible Government alongwith safety and security particularly of tribal people. As a matter of fact, the heavy influx of refugees simply crushed the tribal economy. From the time of partition till the end of 1950, in three years about 1,75,000 displaced persons crossed the border and came to Tripura from East Pakistan. The flow was maximum during the years 1950 and 1952 and 1955-56. Upto 1958, the total number of displaced persons who officially registered themselves as refugees was 3.74 lakhs comprising 83,000 families, of whom about 70,339 families were rendered rehabilitation.[57] By the end of 1957 about 3,65,000 displaced persons came to Tripura and enhanced the total population of the State to the tune of 9,05,000 in 1958 whereas the total population was recorded 6,40 lakhs only.[58] Dr. Ganguly (1968) rightly observes, "Such a large-scale rehabilitation of refugees in the rural areas of Tripura broke to pieces last remnants of isolation enjoyed by the Jhumias."[59] Further the new administration followed the policy of defeating the resistance of tribal people instead of finding a real solution of the problem. Moreover, in the name of the refugees rehabilitation lands of thousands of farmers irrespective of Hindu, Muslim, Tribal or Hindustani communities were requisitioned.[60] However, political organisation like Mukti Parishad and the Communist Party stood against this land requisition policy of the Government and simultaneously raised the demands for granting loan and proper rehabilitation to the refugees. But the Government without caring for socio-psychological problems imposed repressive machinery to restrict the popular movement. In self-defence, the people in the hills i.e., the tribals became united and a feeling of chauvinism clouded the inter-relations of the behaviour pattern of some sections of the tribals, who subsequently formed a secret communal tribal organisation under the banner 'Sen-krak'. There was another tribal organisation commonly known as Tribal Union which was also very much chauvinistic in character. It may be noted in the context that when State Re-organisation Commission (1955) proposed Tripura for inclusion in the Assam State, the 'Tribal Union' welcomed the approach on the ground that such step will restrict Bengali hegemony. Later on, Sankrak formed alliance with the Tribal Union and demanded for a separate Tribal State comprising Meghalaya, Mizoram, Arunachal and Tripura. It is significant to note that such demand was also sponsored by the other hill States of North-east India excepting Nagaland.[61]

The Sino-Indian border dispute of 1962 brought about a big upheaval in the political horizon of India. In 1965 the Communist Party was divided on the issue of Chinese invasion. Those who supported China Policy formed a separate organisation and came to be known as Communist Party (Marxist). In Tripura the leftist tribals formed *Ganamukti Parishad* under the leadership of Communist Party (Marxist) while the rightist tribals formed *Upajati Yuba Samity* under the inspiration of the then ruling Congress Party.

It is thus, evident that instead of belonging to the already existing national parties which are dominated by the Bengalees who are not likely to look after their interests the tribals engaged themselves in organising their own political parties consisting of the tribal peoples alone. The realisation was given concrete shape in the organisation of such parties as *Sankrak*, *Tripura Upajati Samiti*, etc. These organisations were absolutely manned by the tribal peoples alone and their primary object as laid down is to protect the rights and privileges of the tribal communities and to establish an independent tribal State in Tripura. When the Upajati Yuba Samiti was actively engaged in making its own political foundation, the Left Front came to power in 1978. And finally when Left Front came to power, the Upajati Yuba Samiti got the opportunity to mobilise its forces in collaboration with the Congress Party. On the other hand another chauvinistic political organisation viz., *Amra Bangali* was formed being patronised by *Anand-Margis.* Thus two communal organisations which are dimetrically opposite in their ideology overcast the political horizon of Tripura.

Alongwith the formation of these political organisations amongst the tribal peoples, a reference may be made to the significant changes brought about in the tribal economy. The traditional tribal economy became shattered due to the changes brought about by the introduction of advanced techniques of cultivation. It is also to be borne in mind that the tribal people, no doubt, readily acceeded to the introduction of new agricultural techniques, but they have not yet become fully conversant with it in such a way as to produce sufficient crops needed for their subsistence. Again, frequent changes of village sites in search of new *Jhum*-fields have entailed heavy loss of crops. Naturally, the whole tribal economy broke down and the result proved disastrous. They found no other alternative but to borrow money from the money-lenders who are again invariably the non-tribal Bengali Hindus. The money-lenders also charged heavy interest varying from 50 per cent to 100 per cent. Such a high rate of interest made the tribal people unable to repay the debt incurred and as result they had to sell out their lands and other possessions.

Further, after they have been deprived of their land-holdings, most of the tribals have become reduced to servitude working as serfs for their money-lenders or land-holders. Further, the recording of the ownership of the land all over Tripura has been very defective and unsatisfactory. The tribal cultivators have not been recorded as actual owners of the land in the official register. It was also not possible for the tribal people to get their claims officially recorded. This has been clearly stated by the National Committee constituted in 1981 on the development of the tribal areas. It has been stated, "wherever formal land settlement was introduced for the first time or a new settlement was ordered after a long period, it was difficult for the tribal to get his rights recorded." It may also be noted that the ownership of the landed property could be recorded in favour of the tribal cultivators, if only the settlement officers actually did so. As a result, there occurred anomalies in regard to the official recordings and the cultivators of the field. As a consequence of these anomalies in respect of recording ownerships of agricultural lands, the tribes of Tripura are being persistently deprived of their landed property.

In addition to all these factors noted above, other changes have also taken place. With the merger of the State with the Union of India in 1949 all previous orders, rules etc. of the

Maharaja became for all practical purposes ineffective and inoperative. The system of administration in the State was modelled after the all Indian fashion and a positive step was taken towards centralisation and bureaucracy. Not only that, the administration became primarily, manned by the non-tribals. The administration authorities exercising control and implementing all measures from far off places without any experience of the interior and isolated tribal villages in the hills and forests have become less effective. As such, the administration failed to realise the actual grievances, their difficulties and other drawbacks from far off places. Naturally persons with vested interests availed of this opportunity, and accordingly nothing concrete could have been done in respect of mitigating the grievances of the tribals and also of improving their socio-economic conditions.

Economically, the tribal communities of Tripura are bereft of their land and other resources of subsistences. They have been also deprived of their little possessions by the exploiters and as a result, they have become subjected to abject poverty. They are now conscious of large scale exploitation carried out by the non-tribal people in all aspects of their life and activities. All these have also certainly produced great discontent and anger amongst the tribals against both fronts, i.e., Government and non-tribal communities. For all practical purposes their ill-feelings have been primarily directed against the non-tribals who are responsible for running the administration itself This ill-feeling and discontentment amongst the tribals towards the non-tribals have become aggravated by the intervention of the Christian Missionaries who have added fuel to the fire.

The Christian Missions whose sole object has been proselytisation are also largely responsible for instigating the tribal peoples against the non-tribals. They even made the tribals more and more conscious of their language and culture. They have also succeeded in infusing hatred and disregard towards the Bengalees. All these were certainly done by them with the purpose of forming one State over North-eastern region which would in that case remain under their domination and which would certainly play an anti-national role within the Indian Union. That the Christian Missionaries infused deep hatred towards the Bengalees is quite apparent from the demand of the tribal peoples for the replacement of the Bengali Script by the Roman Script for the tribal languages. It may be noted that as the tripals of Tripura like other tribal peoples of India have no script of their own, it was under the patronage of the *Maharaja* that the Bengali script was introduced and the tribal languages are being written in that script. It was, however, at the instance of the Christian Missionaries that the tribals of Tripura, more particularly those who have been made converts to Christianity, have raised the demand for the replacement of the Bengali script.

But those tribals who entertain national feelings and bonds with the Union of India, however, are making an attempt to create a new script of their own for writing their languages. The fact remains that the tribals have been taught to disregard or dishonour the Bengali language or script which was quite popular amongst the tribal peoples of Tripura for a long time past. The tribals have been actually infused with this idea that if the Bengalees could be driven out of the State, it would be then possible for them to from a separate State of their own in Tripura. In this context, a particular reference may be made to a declaration made by a senior leader of the Tribal Union, Mr. S.K. Chakma to the effect that the Bengalees are to be driven-out of the State of Tripura. It is also very interesting to note that Mr. Chakma who was anti-Bengali in the early report of his political life became a staunch supporter of a communal party like *Amra Bangali* within a span of thirty years. Not only that, Mr. Chakma contested in the general election in 1984 as a candidate of *Amra Bangali*.

This long continued and persistent discontent, hatred and anger against the non-tribals of Tripura have taken violent turns in recent years. The tribal peoples have accordingly organised themselves in such a way as to make all out efforts to terrorise the Bengalees in a manner as to compel them to leave the State of Tripura. Subsequently, a convention was held in the month of March, 1978 at Taidu of South Tripura under the banner of *Tripura Upajati Yuba Samiti* (TUJS). It may be noted that the important personalities like Mr. *Bijoy Hrankhwal*, *Rajmahishi Bibhu Devi*, M.L.A. (Cong.) were also present in that convention. The resolution was passed unanimously that all foreigners should be driven out of the State.[62] The popular slogan was *Kachak Kufur Chhumchhiya* ; *buri tata tang lia* ! (We are neither Congress nor Communists. We are for the tribals only).

Mention may be made in this context that Mr. Hrankhawl joined TUJS. He was the Assistant Secretary of the Samity till the formation of TNV. During his association with the Samity, Mr. Hrankhawl came into contact with Laldenga, the Ex-Chief Minister of Mizoram and even wrote in favour of Mizo National Front in the *Tripura Star* urging the necessity of bilateral talks between the Centre and the M.N.F. in the interest of tribals of North-east India.[63] He also convinced the leaders of the TUJS that a Voluntary Organisation of the tribals of Tripura is to be formed for greater interest and accordingly he formed *Tripura Sena*, a purely tribal communal militia. Within ten years since his joining in TUJS i.e. in 1977, Mr. Hrankhawl contested Lok-Sabha seat from East Tripura reserved seat as a TUJS candidate, although he was defeated miserably in that election. In the next Assembly elections he refused to contest and consequently a rift became inevitable with the party command. Mr. Hrankhawl officially declared the formation of T*ribal National Voluntee·s* popularly known as TNV in December, 1978, without the consent of his party. He also became the self-styled supreme commander of the TNV. It may be noted that the original seventy-two members of the TNV were the ex-members of *Tripura Sena* and close associates of Mr. Hrankhwal. This was followed by his expulsion from the TUJS for his illegal activities.

It has already been pointed out that Mr. Hrankhawl have close links with the top leaders of MNF and naturally after the expulsion and formation of a new militia like TNV, he got a free hand in maintaining unholy alliance with the MNF. Without sparing much time Mr. Hrankhawl sent the first terrorist group of TNV comprising fourteen selected members for undergoing weapon training under the guidance of MNF insurgents to Sajak of Chittagong Hill Tracts of Bangladesh. TNV's first attack against the non-tribals was launched in collaboration with the Mizo insurgents in August 1979, that is, within seven months since the formation of TNV. The targets were mainly police-barracks and markets of Amarpur of South Tripura District. The subsequent attack also followed within a span of less than one year. The victimised police stations and markets were Killa, Thelakum, Dulakbazar and Gulirai bazar respectively. The policy of terrorising the non-tribals reached its climax on June 6, 1980 at Mandai village of West Tripura where more than 200 persons were brutally killed. It was such a ghastly measure that the Home Minister of the Government of India had to confess that "India had never before experienced such well planned acts of mass-killing as witnessed in Tripura".[64] The Chief Minister of Tripura also did make a declaration to the effect that the main objective of such a mass killing was to terrorise the Bengali population to leave Tripura.

It may be noted that the *Mandai Massacre* is only the first milestone of the long distant target. This would be evident from the statistical survey of the terrorist activities of Tribal extremists from 1980 onwards as shown in Appendixes-I, II & III.

Now the frequent TNV raids and ruthless massacre of non-tribal civilians in the tribal areas within the autonomous district council resulted in massive exodus of non-tribals from that areas, covering 68 per cent of the State's territory.[65] Further unprecedented spurt in extremist activities and large scale demands for subscriptions by TNV activists administration in Tripura hills was heavily damaged. According to observers, there the massive extortions drive has sparkled speculation that the Tribal National Volunteers have struck a major arms deal with the Bangladesh Security Forces.[66] Again, according to intelligence sources, the extremists were also in touch with private arms dealers in the Chittagong port areas. Cases of unmarked ammunition recovered by the State Police during recent raids in extremist hide-outs confirm that the TNV already had access to foreign arms and ammunition.[67] Naturally, for the large consignment of arms and ammunition the extremists always depend upon subscriptions paid by the non-tribals. Hence, collection drive was not a recent phenomenon.

Many non-tribals did admit that they regularly paid subscriptions for the past few years. The system of collection was that a group of 10 men-collaborators forming squads in each area collected the subscriptions and passed it on to an intermediary to be handed over to the local TNV Commander. Every link in the extortion racket gets a commission, resulting in the exorbitant demands ranging between Rs. 50 to Rs. 20,000. According to Datta (1986), "The fear psychosis created by the extortions was so intense that even Government employees and teachers posted within 15 kms. of the State Capital were afraid to go to work regularly. Almost all Government employees working in the tribal dominated district council areas received notices for exorbitant subscriptions.[68] Intelligence sources said about 20,000 "tax notices" with the seal of the TNV had been issued to both the tribals and non-tribals in the month of November, 1986. Affected people did not seek the help of police because in that case, they knew, they would have to face the killing squads of TNV. Though police personnel were aware of the extortion drives they were helpless and could not prevent it. The Government is also concerned over the massive exodus of non-tribals in as much as thousands of families are in the process of leaving the hill areas from fear of extortion. Under these circumstances, it was, in the long run decided on 6th January, 1987 in New Delhi to designate certain areas of Tripura bordering Bangladesh as "disturbed areas" which were brought under the Armed Forces Special Power Act 1958 in view of the spate of killings by TNV insurgents. The decision however, came at talks between the Home Minister Mr. Buta Singh and the then Chief Minister Mr. Nripen Chakraborty.

It is evident from the above analysis that the TNV is working a definite strategy of driving out non-tribals from the tribal council areas so that the political demand for a union territory and consequently a constituent State status like Mizoram could be raised.

REFERENCES

1. Roy, Jagat Jyoti : *Bidroha Bibartan-O-Tripura*, 1985, p. 28.
2. Stewart, C.: *History of Bengal*, p. 267.
3. Mackenzie, A. : *The North-East Frontier of India* (Reprinted 1979) p. 272.
4. Ganguiy, J.B. : *The Economic Content of the State Formation Process in Medieval Tripura*, p. 151.
5. Roy, Jagat Jyoti : *Op. cit.*, p. 25.
6. Sinha, K.C. : *Rajmala*, 1896, p. 122.
7. Roy Choudhury, N.N. : *Tripura Through the Ages*, p. 122.
8. Sinha, K.C. : *Op. cit.*, p. 25.
9. Roy, Jagat Jyoti : *Op. cit.*, p. 28.
10. *Noakhali District Gazetteers*, p. 23
11. Roy Choudhury, N.N. : *Op. cit.*, p. 53.
12. *Ibid.*
13. Hunter, W. ; *Statistical Account of Bengal.*
14. Roy Choudhury, N.N. : *Op. cit.*
15. *Ibid.*
16. Mackenzie, Sir Alexander : *Op. cit.*, p. 53
17. Sinha, K.C. : *Op cit.*, p. 364.
18. Roy Choudhury, N.N. : *Op. cit.*, p. 64.
19. *Bengal Judicial Proceedings.* A. 26th Sept., 1860 Nos. 357-358.
20. *Ibid.*
21. Mackenzie, A. : *Op. cit*, p. 53-54.
22. *Ibid.*, p. 286
23. Roy Choudhury, N.N. : *Op. cit.*, pp. 67-68.
24. Hunter, W.: *Op cit.*, pp. 508-510
25. *Ibid.*
26. Menon, K.D. : *Tripura District Gazetteers.*
27. Sinha, K.C. : *Op. cit.*, p. 187.
28. Deb, Burma S.C. : *Tripura Census Bibarani*, 1340 T.E.
29. Roy, Jagat Jyoti : *Op. cit.*, p- 48
30. Ganguly, J.B. : *Op. cit.*, p. 156.
31. *Ibid.*
32. *The Proceedings of the Shashan Sanmilani*, 1913 A.D. p. 7
33. Roy Burman, B.K. : *Demographic and Socio-economic Profiles of the Hill Areas of North-Eastern India*, New Delhi, 1970.

34. *Ibid.*
35. Menon, K.D. : *Op cit.*, p. 160.
36. Datta, Biren : *Prajar Katha Weekly Bengali 15th Baisakh*, 1349 T.E.
37. Menon, K.D. : *Op cit.*,
38. Chakraborty, M. : *Communist Activities in Tripura 1939-42* (Proceedings of N.E. India History Association).
39. Deb Burma, A. : *Tripura Desh in Bengali* (1st Issue.) Agartala 24th Oct, 1972.
40. Menon, K.D. : *Op. cit.*, p. 126.
41. *Ibid.*
42. *Ibid.*
43. Ganguly, J.B. : *Op. cit.*, p. 62
44. Roy Choudhury, N.N. : *Op. cit.*, p. 88
45. *Ibid.* p. 91.
46. *Ibid.*,
47. Majumder, B.M.: *The Struggle for Responsible Government in Tripura* (1947-1956).
41. Roy Choudhury, N.N.: *Op. cit.*, p. 95.
49. *Ibid.*
50. *Ibid.*
51. Roy, Jagat Jyoti : *Op. cit.*
52. Datta, Biren : *Amar Smritite Tripurar Communist Andolan-O-Ganatantrik Andoloner Patabhumika*
53. Roy, Jagat Jyoti : *Op. cit.*, p. 56.
54. Majumder, B.M. : *Op. cit.*, p. 419.
55. *Ibid.*
56. Roy Choudhury, N.N. : *Op cit.*,
57. Menon, K.D. : *Op. cit*
58. Ganguly, J.B. : *Op. cit.*, pp. 69-70.
59. *Ibid.*
60. Sen, Tripur Chandra : *Tripura in Transition Agartala*, 1970 p. 24.
61. *Tripura Darpan Saradiya*, 1391 p. 14.
62. *Ibid.*
63. Bhowmik, S. : *Parbatua Jibaner Jangi Manasikata*, Agartala (Tripura Darpan, 1986) p. 15
64. *Amrita Bazar Patrika*, Calcutta 13th June, 1980.
65. *The Statesman*, Calcutta 15th June, 1980.
66. Datta, S. : *The Telegraph*, Calcutta, 11th December, 1986.
67. *Ibid.*, 13th December, 1986.
68. *Ibid.*,

SEVEN

POLITICAL ASPECTS OF THE EXTREMISTS

A cursory glance at the map of India and Bangladesh will show why Tripura had to receive a large proportion of refugees. The State being surrounded by Bangladesh on three sides and having a common border with the districts of Chittagong, Noakhali, Comilla and Sylhet, Tripura is the easiest place of migration of minority community of Bangladesh during the periods of political or communal disharmony. References may be made to the first and the second batch of evacuees migrated to Tripura after the unprecedented Dacca communal riots of 1941 and Noakhali riots of 1946 respectively. Subsequently, after the partition of India on communal basis, the evacuees, that is, the victims of the partition in their thousands poured into this adjacent tiny State, even smaller than any district of West Bengal, brought about a demographic revolution in the State and simultaneously reduced the tribal people to a minority community in their own homeland. But the most humanitarian aspect was that the tribes of Tripura initially, did not react to rehabilitation of the refugees rather they shared their sorrows and sufferings.

But unfortunately, the humanitarian approach of the tribals could not survive for long. They found that they were struggling for their own existence. As a matter of fact, rehabilitation of the victims of the partition was unplanned and faulty and as a result of which the tribals of Tripura had to pay dearly. To understand the issue involved, it would probly be wise to refer to the land revenue system of Tripura. It is significant to note that till 1880, there was no regular land revenue system in Tripura. It is only after 1880, a number of acts and rules came into force in the princely State. In this land revenue system a class of intermediaries was created between the tiller of the land who held land under the system 'Kayemi Taluk', 'Tashkhichi Taluk', 'Niskar Taluk' and 'Jotes'.[1] This land revenue system was applicable to those cultivators who had taken to settled cultivation, that is, mostly the non-tribal Bengalees. Naturally, the tribals who practised 'Jhum' or shifting cultivation were beyond the jurisdiction of the above land revenue system. It was Maharaja Bir Bikram (1923-47) who was wise enough to recognise the need for protecting the interests of the tribal people, and created reserved areas for them covering around 42 per cent of the area of the State.

The fact cannot be denied that after the merger of the State with the Indian union and with the formation of new democratic government in Tripura, the administration urgently took up the problem of refugee rehabilitation on a war-footing and at the same time it was also true for a democratically elected government to be extra cautious about vote-catching policy. The result was that the tribal reserved areas were not spared but infiltrated by the non-tribal refugees. It was, indeed, unfortunate that in the name of rehabilitation the then State Government requisitioned land of even farmers belonging to the Hindu, Muslims, tribals and Hindusthani communities and even the grazing grounds of the tribals were not spared.[3] It may be noted again, in this context, that with the attainment of independence in 1947, followed by heavy influx of refugees from erst-while East Pakistan (now Bangladesh), a National Conference was held under the leadership of Prime Minister Pandit Nehru in 1952 for discussing the problems of Scheduled Tribes and Scheduled Castes. Shri Dasarath Deb, the then Lok Sabha member from Tripura categorically stated, "Some area or areas of Tripura shall have to be set aside for the tribal alone and no other persons belonging to non-tribal communities should be allowed to settle there. And this conference should take note that this is not a new idea at all".[4] Subsequently tribal organisation like Gana Mukti Parishad in their memorandum to Pandit Nehru stated. "In the present scramble for land, it is not possible for the tribals, particularly for the tribal jhumias, to secure land on personal initiative. Therefore, in the area inhabited by tribal people, all 'khas' land should be reserved exclusively for the rehabilitation of tribals."[5]

These developments were thus unwelcome and undesirable. The tribal people who live in rural hilly areas and derive their livelihood from land only, landlessness caused not only a sense of disappointment among them but also created socio-political instability in the State. Now, the tribals, failing to bear the gross injustice, they tried to resist the move by launching a political movement. Meanwhile, with the merger of the State with the Indian Union, waves of political activities also reached in this tiny State and a new political horizon emerged in the life and activities of the tribals of Tripura.

It is interesting to note that instead of alignment with the existing national political parties which are dominated by the non-tribals and who are not likely to lookafter their interest, the tribals engaged themselves in organising their own political parties consisting of the tribal peoples alone. This realisation was given concrete shape in the organisation of such parties like Santisena-Bahini (1949), Sengkrack (1949), Paharia Union (1951), Adivasi Samity (1952), Tripura Rajya Adivasi Sangha (1953), Adivasi Sansad (1954), Upajati Yuba Samity (1967), Tripura-National Volunteers (1978), Army of Tripura Peoples' Liberation Organisation (1980), Tripura Hills People Party (1983) etc.[7] Since the primary concern of these organisations was to protect the rights and privileges of the tribal communities of the State, they finally took a leaf out of Assam's book to demand expulsion of all those who had settled in the State after October, 1949.[6] It would not be irrelevent to note that in this regard, some foreign hands specially Christian organisations played a dominant role in instigating the tribals to act violently against the non-tribals for fulfilling their political aspirations.

This will be evident from the Parliamentary records that the Ministry of Home Affairs, Government of India in a letter to the State Government dated 29th May, 1953 asked to furnish information so that a comparison could be made between the number of Foreign Missions who entered India during a five year period immediately before and after the 15th August, 1947. The State Report[7] shows that since the period from 1938 to 1953 there were three Foreign Missionaries viz. New Zealand Baptist Mission, Agartala, New Zealand Baptist Mission, Bhangmung in the Jampui Hills and Roman Catholic Mission at Mariamnagar, Agartala. It has also been reported that immediately after 15th August, 1947 two more foreign missionaries were set up in Tripura viz., New Zealand Baptist Mission at Dhuma Chhera under Kailasahar sub-division and American Baptist Mission at Dharmanagar. The name of the New Zealand Baptist Mission, however, in the later period was changed into Tripura Baptist Christian Union (TBCU). According to recent survey work, it has been observed that at present five Christian organisations are working in Tripura.[8] They are: Tripura Baptist Christian Union, Zeraw Baptist Mission of Mizoram, Roman Catholic Church, United Protestant Church of North-East India and Evangelical Free Church of India. It is important to note that the Tripura Baptist Christian Union have a common Forum in the North-East India Christian Council (NEICC) with its headquarter in Shillong. The NEICC is again affiliated to Dr. Billy Graham's World Baptist Alliance.[9] It is also to be noted excepting the Roman Catholic Church, the remaining four organisations are run by Tribal Christian Missionaries of Tripura, Manipur and Mizoram.

All these missionaries have profound socio-political influence on the tribals due to their welfare activities particularly in the field of education and medical treatment. Side by side, the Christian missionaries offered socio-religious and political lessons to the young converts who are subsequently promoted to the rank of 'Pastor' as the path-finder to the tribal societies. In fact, the Pastors are not only the spiritual advisers but also the socio-political leaders of the tribal society and it was at their instance, the tribal extremists raised the demand for Roman script in the place of Bengali script which has been quite popular amongst the tribal peoples of Tripura for a long time past. The fact also remains that the Christian missions are largely responsible for militant activities being connected with the large movement covering the entire area of North-eastern India where also the tribal peoples are making all out efforts to establish their own political authority.

Regarding the involvement of the Christian missionaries with the political arena of the extremists mention may be made that the Dinesh Singh Committee which visited Tripura from 13 to 18 July, 1980 observes : this was a limited significance only in comparison with far more overt missionary activity in the rest of the North-East region... Even among the Christian missions, it is only the Tripura Baptist Christian Union (TBCU) that has come to adverse notice because of the subscriptions they receive from abroad, and because of the political links with the tribal extremists. Besides, a pamphlet entitled "The Church grows through people's movement", circulated mainly among the church authorities in North-Eastern India on the eve of the Mandai massacre (June, 1980) gives the impression that there is a close relation, between tribal political movement and conversion.

The pamphlet runs : The political upheaval has made the tribals of Tripura receptive to the Gospel. If large numbers are to come to Christ via peoples' movement, the Tripura Baptist Christian Union must be aided by other churches and missions.[11] Dr. Ricwch Cunville, who was the author and also the Director of the Bible Society of India says, "the desire to obey Christ's Great Commission at this crucial stage in the life of the peoples of Tripura must burn away all our denominational differences. I strongly feel (I) the door to be opened for any Christian denomination to cater and evangelize the Tripuris (2) where with the TBCU so that the caring and perfecting be done together with the TBCU and (3) all Churches to support and loan their best men and women for discipling of the Tripuris as far as possible under the direction of the TBCU. This is the ideal method. Along with this third recommendation, I also strongly urge the pumping into Tripura of material supplies—jeeps, public address systems. Tracts and printing materials to be used by the workers in their thirst for Christ among the Tripuris.[12]

It is, thus, clear from the above documentary evidences that Christianity is gradually and steadily making inroads into the tribal society of Tripura, introducing a new kind of leadership based on political and religious manoeuvers. References may be made in this context to Bijoy Kumar Hrangkhawl, a young converted christian of the Kuki sub-tribe who was the Assistant General Secretary of the Tripura Upajati Juba Samity (TUJS). His aggressive style of functioning and intimate contact with the church brought him in direct conflict with the devout Hindu Tripuri and Jamatia leadership. They had dominant position in the organisation and naturally within short notice the TUJS leadership sacked Hrangkhawl. He now got the free hand because the situation paved the way to move in his own choice. Hrangkhawl openly disclosed about the formation of the Tripura National Volunteers popularly known as TNV on 10th October, 1978 and his involvement with the Bangladesh trained tribal boys who raided Amarpur under the leadership of Mizo National Front (MNF) in 1979. Hrangkhawl's policy was to make all out effort to terrorise the Bengalees in a manner so as to compel them to leave the State. In his own statement he confessed : "To be frank I followed nobody. My political understanding of Tripura came out of my practical study, out of my own conviction. The situation in Tripura is a little different from that in other parts of the North-East. Take Nagaland, Mizoram. The lands are their own, of the Mizoram people, the Naga people. Even if Laldenga is not the Chief Minister, it is all the same because all are Mizos. But our case in Tripura is different".[13]

From the above frank confession, it is almost clear about the political manoeuvery of the extremists. The motive being to make Tripura a tribal dominant State by driving out the non-tribals from the land. Hence, the policy of terrorising the non-tribals necessarily took the violent forms in the nature of destruction of life and property of non-tribals. It is also evident that the extremists ideology was purely based on communal militancy scrupulously avoiding any conflict with the national main stream. But the so-called liberation war against the refugees has not carried that much of popular support because a good number of tribals in the past even did not hesitate to fight for the cause of the refugees on humanitarian grounds. In support of this statement, mention may be made that the tribal leaders like Birbhadra Tripura, and Dasarath Noatia even expressed solidarity by joining the Refugee hunger strike at Sonamura sub-division of Tripura.[14] It was argued that the rehabilitation of the victims of the partition in Tripura would not jeopardise the interests of the tribal people. Rather the rehabilitation of such refugees in Tripura having abundant fallow land, the most part of which was full of dense jungles and forests where nothing but wild animals roamed about freely, would auger development in Tripura by augmenting not only, Government revenues but also production in the State.[15]

The consensus was that side by side with the task of refugee rehabilitation, the administration should also take proper steps to redress the privations and grievances of the tribal people undertaking tribal development schemes. Interestingly, commoners of both the communities, that is, tribals and non-tribals mutually shared their sorrows and sufferings and also put emphasis on the tribal and non-tribal unity for a joint movement for redressal of grievances of both the communities.[16] The fact thus, remains that the militant approach of the extremists was not heartily accepted by the simple peace loving people of the tribal communities but unfortunately due to such rejection on their part, many of them unnecessarily became the hit targets of oppression both physically and mentally. However, Government's appeal for bringing back the extremists to the national mainstream was quite responsive.

A good number of extremists surrendered to the humanitarian call by the Government. Bijoy Kumar Hrangkhawl, the supreme commander of the TNV also had a series of talks with Nripen Chakraborty, former Chief Minister of

Tripura and it has been observed that since then out of disappointment he was contemplating to surrender along with Shri Binanda Jamatia, another extremist leader of the Army of Tripura Peoples' Liberation Organisation (ATPLO) in the hill tracts of Chittagong. But Hrangkhawl's fate was written otherwise. By this time, he was kidnapped by Binanda Jamatia who confined him forcefully to his militant camp in the Chittagong hill tracts of Bangladesh. Subsequently, Chuni Kalai, a right hand lieutenant of Bijoy Hranghkhawl over powered Binanda group and freed him. Hrangkhwal again went back to his past life raising the militant slogan "Tripura for Tripuris". Meanwhile, Binanda joined the Tribal Ganamukti Parishad (1983) backed by C.P.I.(M) Party along with 183 extremists in response to the policy of "appeasing and winning over the extremists" followed by the Left Front Government in 1980. It was believed that Binanda was responsible for forming "Lama Kautul" meaning the 'new change' at the instance of the ruling Left Front Government to act as counter-force against the TNV. But Binanda could not survive. He was mysteriously murdered by unknown assassins. Meanwhile, on 10th January, 1986 Bijoy Hrangkhawl addressed Rajiv Gandhi hailing him as a great leader.[18] Two years later, a tripartite agreement was signed in New Delhi on August, 1988 by the Central Government, newly elected Cong(I)-TUJS coalition Government of the State and the outlawed TNV extremists (1988).

It is significant to note that in the Preamble to the Memorandum of Understanding (MUS), it has been observed : The Tripura National Volunteer (TNV) through their letter dated 4th May, 1988, addressed to the Governor of Tripura and signed by Shri Bijoy Kumar Hrangkhawl stated that keeping in view, the Prime Minister, Shri Rajiv Gandhi's policy of solution of problems through negotiations, TNV have decided to abjure violence, give up secessionist demand and to hold negotiations for a peaceful solution of all the problems of Tripura within the Constitution of India.[19] Thus, the sudden change of attitude by the leader of the extremists from underground politicizing secessionist demand, that is, "Swadhin

Tripura" to abjuring violence and accepting Rajiv Gandhi as a great leader, still remains a puzzling quiz in the chess board of Tripura politics.

The accord quite naturally, raised a political storm, with the former CPI(M) Chief Minister Nripen Chakraborty alleging that the accord proved that TNV was a Cong(I) tool although the present Chief Minister Sudhir Ranjan Majumder retorted by terming it as a "ridiculous political propaganda."[20] It is also to be noted in this context that on the Memorandum of Settlement with the TNV, Shri Shyamacharan Tripura, the President of the Tripura Upajati Juba Samity (TUJS) and also the Vice-Chairman of the seven member coordinating committees with representatives from the Cong(I) and the TUJS which provides broad policy guidelines to the present coalition Government, seathingly commented, "Bijoy has surrendered unconditionally. What he has got in the accord is less than what is contained in a tribal sub-plan. For instance, the tribals in Tripura are already getting subsidised rations for five months during the lean period, and the accord promises them three months of subsidised rations. He obviously did not know what he was signing. It is a complete sellout."[21]

Hrangkhawl, however, confesses that there are many unwritten aspects in the accord. According to him, the interests and demands of the tribal people are very simple. The tribals have received so little in the last so many years that they are happy with what little has been given in the accord. Whatever, has been done for the tribals has been because of their struggle. He believes that the Autonomous District Council (ADC) came into being because of their struggle. Hrangkhawl also reiterates that as per unwritten understandings of the accord, "there are to be centres for providing training to tribal people to engage in business, trades. For this, there will be separate committees comprising representatives of the Government of India, the Government of Tripura and the TNV to monitor. We have asked for at least five thousand young tribal men and women to be provided training in different trades, in different parts of the country...All this is not on record, it is one of those unwritten understandings".[22]

The terms of the accord were, however, quite surprising. Besides monetary compensation, the militants got a bunch of promises only. For Hrangkhwal, of course, the considerations were different. He knew very well that the extremists movement had its limitations too. The extremists were only a minute fraction of the people. The strength of active members is less than 200 persons.[23] Though their militant activities started at various sub-divisions of Tripura like Dharmanagar, Amarpur, Kamalpur, Khowai, Belonia, Kailasahar, yet Amarpur was the main centre of activities. So the movement was somewhat localised and Amarpur—based in character. Above all, the general aloofness of the simple peace loving tribals was conspicuous. Hrangkhawl also realised that time was running out and his dream of political career was fading out. At that time, since the opportunity was at the door, it was wise for him to grab at it somehow. Finally, he tookover the offer of Chairmanship of the Tribal Jhumia Rehabilitation and Plantation Corporation with cabinet status. However, from being a little known evangelist, the militant leader has come a long way.[24]

Thus, after the accord, the extremists had two alternatives. First, to trun the militants into a full fledged party and secondly, to merge the militants with the TUJS. Probably, Hrangkhawl favours to merge his TNV militants with the TUJS. In support of this statement Hrangkhawl's own observation about TUJS deserves worth mentioning. He says : "They (TUJS) are very good to me and to us. I am grateful to them. Moreover, most of the supporters of the TUJS are my supporters and my supporters are TUJS. We cannot distinguish between the two".[25] It is very interesting from political point of view that Shyama Charan Tripura's attitude towards Hrangkawl is also not antagonistic. On Hrangkhawl's future political plans, he emphatically stated, "We do not mind him joining the TUJS. I have already invited him to join our party though our experience with him has not been happy. But let me also confess that if the TNV joins the TUJS, especially if Bijoy joins, we may have problems. But if he floats the TNV as a political party, there will be no problems. Whatever, glamour he may have had as the leader of an insurgency has vanished after signing the accord. The tribal youth cannot be decieved".[26]

The recent combined alliance of the Cong(I), TUJS and TNV at the time of Tripura's Tribal Areas Autonomous District Council's election (July, 1990) against the Left Front led by CPI(M) amply justifies speculated political trend of the TNV extremists. Again, the success of the Cong (I), TUJS alliance in the election also suggests that the Leftists have failed to recover their setback in the State Assembly polls about two years back. In fact, the decline of the Marxist's influence in the tribal areas of Tripura is probably the most intriguing feature of the State's politics because they represented the most powerful political force encompassing the tribal communities of Tripura in the early fifties and sixties.

REFERENCES

1. Sinha, A : *Tribal Landlessness and Social Discontent in Tripura : An Analysis of the Economic Background.* (The paper was submitteed in the Seminar on Social Movement in Societies of Tripura, Feb., 1990).
2. *Ibid.*
3. Sen, Tripur : Tripura in Transition ; Agartala, 1970.
4. Memorandum submitted to the Eighth Finance Commission by Tripura Tribal Areas Autonomous District Council, Agartala p. 1.
5. *Ibid.*
6. The Statesman, 12th June, 1980.
7. Chakraborty, M : *Growth of Christianity in Tripura and some Tribal Movements since Independence* (Seminar paper).
8. *Ibid.*
9. *Ibid.*
10. *Ibid.*
11. *Ibid.*
12. *Ibid*
13. *Ibid.*
14. Mohanta, B : The Refugee Rehabilitation Movement in Tripura (1950-1960). (Seminar paper).
15. *Ibid.*
16. Resolution of the All Tripura Refugee Convention held on 3-4 February, 1951-published in 'Janakalyan'. Agartala, 1951.

17. Roy, Jagatjyoti : *Bidroha Bibartan-O-Tripura*, *Tripura Darpan Prakashani*, Agartala, 1985.
18. *Parivartan* 24-30 August (in Bengali), Calcutta, August, 1988.
19. *Front Line*. September, 17-30, 1988.
20. *India Today*, September, 15, 1988.
21. *Frontline* : September, 17-30, 1988.
22. *Ibid.*
23. *Ibid.*
24. Menon, R : Hasty Pact ; Published in India Today, September, 15, 1988.
25. *Front Line*, September, 17-30, 1988.
26. *Ibid.*

EIGHT

TNV's INSURGENT ACTIVITIES AND THE PEACE ACCORD

The emergence of the Tripura Upajati Juba Samiti (TUJS) in 1967 was, in fact, a natural corollary to the socio-political upheavals in the State and since then the party had been steadily and radically altering the State's political landscape. Subsequently, some orthodox Bengalees also formed *Amra Bangali* on a communal basis as a counter organisation to fight for their rights. Meanwhile the communal polarisation reached its climax when the TUJS and *Amra Bangali* divided between amongst over 28 per cent of the votes in the Lok-Sabha election held in the month of January, 1980.

It may be noted that in the weeklong convention of TUJS at *Kantyakubra para* in Sadar Sub-division in June, 1967, the veteran tribal leaders like Dasarath Deb of CPI(M) and Aghore Deb Burma of CPI were also present as the party representatives. But both the leaders boycotted the TUJS almost instantly on the ground that the ideology of the new born party was based on communal militancy. In the above convention, the TUJS, however, unanimously adopted 'the eleven points' charter of demands including the extension of the fifth schedule in Tripura, introduction of Kokborok language as the medium of instruction for tribal students and restoration of alienated tribal lands.[1] The organisational network was made of tribal students, women and employees. A voluntary armed wing viz., 'Tripura Sena' was also formed in 1971 under the leadership of Bishnu Deb Burma, a retired army Havaldar.

The Party leadership of the TUJS was deeply concerned with the lack of representation from the tribal communities like the Halam, Kuki, Lushai, etc. The Party, therefore, recruited Bijoy Hrangkhawl, a tribal Christian of Halam community to fill the vacuum. Hrangkhawl also spared no time to come to the forefront and very soon he became the Assistant General Secretary of the Party. Some of the party leaders, however, were not very happy with him for his over ambitious role in the inner line of the party organisation. The Party also faced a crisis following disclosures about the secret formation of Tripura National Volunteers (TNV) by Bijoy Hrangkhawl. The moderate leaders of the TUJS took exception to his involvement in the raid on Amarpur in August, 1979 by his Bangladesh trained boys in collaboration with the Mizo National Front (MNF) extremists. Naturally, the party thought that it would be wise to severe connection with Hrangkhawal. Meanwhile, the CPI (M) Government enacted a legislation providing for establishing a Tribal Autonomous District Council in Tripura. The Bill sought to create an autonomous tribal region within Tripura comprising 7, 132.56 sq. kms out of a total of 10,447 sq. kms, which will be governed by an elected Council comprising 21 tribal and 7 non-tribal members.[2]

Although, in general, tribals of all communities welcomed the Bill, the Tripura Upajati Juba Samiti (TUJS) and particularly the militants among the tribals criticised it and demanded in its place district council under the sixth schedule of the Constitution according to which the Council would have been directly responsible to the Central Government, through the Governor of the State. The Tripura Tribal Areas Autonomous District Council Bill, 1979, however, received the President's assent on 20 July, 1979. According to unofficial estimates about 70 per cent of the population of the autonomous district council (Appendix I) will consist of tribals in absolute terms, of the 4,72,290 people estimated to be living in the proposed autonomous district 3,37,073 will be tribals and 1,35,217 from other categories mainly Bengalis.[3] *Amra Bangali* raised the objection that the enactment hands over 75 per cent of the area in Tripura to 25 per cent of its population. But according to Government report out of 10,477 sq. kms. of the State area, the total area of the Tripura Tribal Areas Autonomous District Council is 7,132.56 kms. i.e. 68.10 per cent of the total area of the State. Secondly, Section 35 of the Act empowers the District Council to regulate and control trading within the district. No non-tribal shall be able to carry on wholesale or retail business in any commodity in the district except under a licence issued by the Council.[4] Thirdly, District Council will "prescribe the language and the manner in which primary education shall be imparted in the Primary Schools in the district."[5] This implies that Bengali need not be the medium of instruction in the Primary Schools in the district.

It is, thus, contended that this legislation generated strife between the tribals and the non-tribals. The Bengali community apprehended that once they were driven out from erstwhile East Pakistan and due to the enactment of the new Bill they might be uprooted again. They raised the slogan, "Come let us pledge that we will give life but not allow a partition of Tripura." On the otherhand, the TUJS declared, "It is a question of our survival. Either they (The Bengalis) survive or we". It is, in this way, the peaceful Tripura plunged into a mass orgy of violence. On the 17th January, *Amra Bangali* gave a call for "Tripura Bandh" to register its protest against the District Council Bill. The whole of the plains was by and large affected by the 'Bandh Call'. Violence erupted not only in Sadar sub-division but in other sub-divisions as well. The tribal militants also under the banner of TNV launched armed struggle for the independence of Tripura.

Hrangkhawl, the rebel TUJS leader set up an armed training camp in Chittagong hill tracts of Bangladesh and started preparation for launching an armed struggle for Tripura's independence. He became the self-styled Commander-in-Chief of the *Tripura Sena*. At the same time he was also the President of Tripura Tribal National Front—the political arm of the *Tripura Sena*. The training was given to the extremist tribal youths of Tripura in collaboration with the outlawed

Mizo National Front (MNF). About 60 misguided youths from Tripura were reported to be undergoing training in Bangladesh. But Hrangkhawl could not escape himself from the eyes of the Government. He was arrested on 13th June, 1980 immediately after the Mandai Massacre. As soon as the report came into air, tribal sentiment grew strong. There was public demand from the tribals of Teliamura that Hrangkhawl should be released immediately. Government, however, yielded to that demand and relased him in no time.

It is interesting to note that though Hrangkhawl had not that much of political support but subsequently, tribal sentiment went in his favour because of the fact that when Police force started oppressing innocent tribals in the hilly areas in the name of quelling down the TNV, the hilly people offered resistance against the Government machinery. They thought it wise to support TNV than to be oppressed by the Police force. It was a big opportunity, no doubt for the TNV guerillas to motivate the tribals but they could do nothing because their leaders were more interested in personal achievement than the welfare of the tribal communities as a whole. Naturally, when Nripen Chakraborty, the then Chief Minister of Tripura held three rounds of talks with Hrangkhawl with a desire to bring him back to the main stream he was not totally unconvinced. He got married and started his normal family life with his newly married wife Linda. According to press information, many high officials of the Government of Tripura were present in his marriage ceremony at Ambasha. Not only that, Local Gramin Bank sanctioned huge loan in his favour for opening a rice mill. His village was electrified and roads were constructed and metalled within a short time.[6]

Hrangkhawl had a desire to start a Cinema Hall in Ambasha and for that he applied for license to the authority concerned. But his destiny had decided otherwise. On the 14th August, 1982, Hrangkhawl alongwith his wife Linda were kidnapped by a militant group of ATPLO (Army of Tripura Peoples Liberation Organisation) under the leadership of Binanda Jamatia from his Ambasha residence. Jamatia detained him in an ATPLO's camp located in the hill tracts of Chittagong of Bangladesh. Subsequently, Hrangkhawl was freed by his trusted Lieutenant Chuni Kalai who overpowered the guards of the camp. Thus, Hrangkhawl again came back to his early militant life. With a new zeal he formed a Government named as 'Peoples Democratic Republic of Tripura' and he himself became its President. Meanwhile, Jamatia, the leader of the ATPLO (another militant group of TNV) surrendered to the Government of Tripura and joined the *Uyajati Ganamukti Parishad*. It was a set-back for the TNV militants but Hrangkhawl kept his morale high. As the President of PDRT (Peoples Democratic Republic of Tripura) he declared that people who migrated to Tripura after 15th October, 1949 are to be treated as foreigners. He also wrote a letter to Indira Gandhi stating that tribal liberation movement in Tripura should not be considered isolated from that of the mass upsurge throughout the whole of North-east India.[7] In his own words Hrangkhawl says, "From 1981 and onwards, I conducted insurgency for about eight years, but I was physically present with the insurgency from 1982 when I was taken away by force".[8]

It was almost a regular feature of the TNV guerillas to storm villages and fire indiscriminately irrespective of women and children and immediately after the operation they slipped into their headquarter at Thangong (Map 4) in the Chittagong hill tracts. According to satistical report, a record of 600 people were killed mostly non-tribals during the period of eight years from 1980.[9] Most horrible was the violence that rocked Tripura in June, 1980. According to the State Chief Minister Nripen Chakraborty, over 1800 persons were reported missing, many of them might be dead. Over 34,660 huts were burnt, and loss of property was tentatively estimated at around Rs. 21 crores. A large number of families lost all they had and were forced to seek shelter in camps. The total number of persons who entered relief camps was about 3 lakhs, even after the return of 1.54 lakh persons to their villages under Police protection, there were still about 1.63 lakh inmates (0.43 lakh tribes and 1.20 lakh non-tribals) on 31.7.80 in relief camps set up by the Government.[10]

The law and order situation of the State deteriorated to a no-return stage. P. Chidambaram, the then Union Minister of State for Home Affairs arrived at Agartala on December 28, 1986. He was accompanied by the Union Minister of State for Communications. Santosh Mohan Deb and the State Governor-General K.V. Krishna Rao and other top central officials. The Central team held two hour long meeting with Nripen Chakraborty, the former Chief Minister of the State.

All the members in the meeting reached a consensus to combat the extremists. It was reported that both the Congress(I) and the TUJS delegations submitted memorandum to the Central team demanding the immediate extension of the Disturbed Areas Act, banning of the TNV under the unlawful Activities Prevention Act and also induction of the Army to combat the TNV menace. But Chakraborty refused to accept any proposal from the Centre for extending the purview of the Disturbed areas Act and banning the TNV on the ground that such administrative measures would mean placing the tribals at the mercy of the army. Subsequently, however, both the Chief Minister and the Union Home Minister agreed jointly to designate certain areas of Tripura bordering Bangladesh as "disturbed areas" in view of the spate of killings by TNV insurgents. Meanwhile, the insurgent movement led by Bijoy Hrangkhawl had been marked by intense bloodshed which accounted for over 300 lives in the past three years. Indiscriminate killings, however, had not paid any dividend apart from causing an exodus of non-tribals from the tribal dominated areas. Later on, the killing of two tribals in a retaliatory attacks by the non-tribals made the TNV leadership feel that such massacre of non-tribals would deprive them of their support base even among tribals. Naturally, a change of strategy was evolved at an emergency meeting of the TNV High Command on April 10, 1987.[11] Sources also said that the above meeting decided to go in for selective killings, abductions and sabotage operations to mount pressure on the Centre. As a part of the new strategy, the rebels would also try to kidnap senior Government officials.[12] This is evident from the abduction of the CPI(M) M.L.A. Lean Prasad Molsui from his residence in North District on May 13, 1987.

Just before the Assembly election of Tripura, Rajiv Gandhi came to Tripura as a part of his election campaign. The report goes that when Gandhi was heading towards Kamalpur of North Tripura District by air for attending election meetings the TNV guerillas raided a non-tribal spot which was only a few kilometres away from election meeting. Gandhi addressed the gathering with an emphasis over law and order situation of the State. He blamed the Left Front Government for its failure to tackle the situation effectively. After his return to New Delhi, the Centre declared the whole State as disturbed and inducted the armed forces in a massive way. There was no more guerilla activities by the TNV extremists in the State. Meanwhile, after the general election a new Ministry under the combined leadership of Congress (I) and TUJS led front was sworn in. It was found a militant group of discontented tribals who had murdered about 600 Bengalis in eight years suddenly agreed to surrender within 13 weeks of talks amongst the Centre, the Tripura Government and the Tribal National Volunteers (TNV). And, the Government which was determined to crush the TNV extremists offered a generous rehabilitation package of Rs. 25,000 each to those who would come overground.[13]

There is, however, no doubt that after several rounds of secret negotiations and discussion Bijoy Hrangkhawl and five other TNV leaders signed the 'Memorandum of Understanding' on behalf of the Tribal National Volunteers (TNV) and P. Srivastav, Additional Secretary to the Government of India, Ministry of Home Affairs in presence of General K.V. Krishna Rao (Retd.) Governor of Tripura and Sudhir Ranjan Majumder, Chief Minister of Tripura. Mention may be made that the accord signed by the Tripura National Volunteers in New Delhi on 12th August, 1988, in fact, made little concessions to its original demands. The Memorandum of Understanding amongst the Centre, the State Government and the Tripura National Volunteers is as follows.[14]

MEMORANDUM OF UNDERSTANDING

Preamble

Government of India have been making efforts to bring about a satisfactory settlement of the problems of tribals in Tripura by restoring peace and harmony in areas where disturbed conditions prevailed.

2. The Tripura National Volunteer (TNV) through their letter dated the 4th May, 1988 addressed to the Governor of Tripura and signed by Shri Bijoy Kumar Hrangkhawl, stated that keeping in view the Prime Minister, Shri Rajiv Gandhi's policy of solution of problems through negotiations. TNV have decided to abjure violence, give up secessionist demand and to hold negotiations for a peaceful solution of all the problems of Tripura within the Constitution of India. The TNV also furnished its bye-laws which conform to the laws in force. On this basis a series of discussions were held with representatives of TNV.

3. The following were the outcome of the discussions : Deposit of arms and ammunition and ending of underground activities by TNV :

3.1 The TNV undertakes to take all necessary steps to end underground activities and to bring out all undergrounds of the TNV with their arms, ammunition and equipment within one month of signing of this Memorandum. Details for giving effect to this part of Settlement will be worked out and implemented under the supervision of the Central Government. The TNV further undertakes to ensure that it does not resort to violence and to help in restoration of amity between different sections of the population.

3.2 The TNV undertakes not to extend any support to any other extremist groups by way of training, supply of arms or providing protection or in any other manner.

Rehabilitation of Undergrounds

3.3 Suitable steps will be taken for the resettlement and rehabilitation of TNV undergrounds coming overground in the light of the schemes drawn up for the purpose.

Measures to Prevent Infiltration

3.4 Stringent measures will be taken to prevent infiltration from across the border of strengthening arrangements on the border and constructions of roads along vulnerable sections of the Indo-Bangladesh border in Tripura sector for better patrolling and vigil. Vigorous action against such infiltrators would also be taken under the law.

Reservation of Seats in the Tripura Legislative Assembly for Tribals

3.5 With a view to satisfying the aspirations of tribals of Tripura for a greater share in the governance of the State, legislative measures will be taken including those for the enactment of the Bill for the amendment of the Constitution. The Constitution amendments shall provide that notwithstanding anything contained in the Constitution, the number of seats in the Legislative Assembly of Tripura reserved for Scheduled Tribes shall be such number of seats as bears to the total number of seats, a proportion not less than the number, as on the date of coming into force of the Constitution amendment, of members belonging to the Scheduled Tribes in the existing Assembly bears to the total number of seats in the existing Assembly. The Representation of the People Act, 1950 shall also be amended to provide for reservation of 200 seats for the Scheduled Tribes in the Assembly of Tripura. However, the amendments shall not affect any representation in the existing Assembly of Tripura until its dissolution.

Restoration of Alienated Lands to Tribals

3.6 It was agreed that following measures will be taken:

(i) Review of rejected applications for restoration of tribal land under the Tripura Land Revenue and Land Reforms Act, 1960.

(ii) Effective implementation of the law for restoration.

(iii) Stringent measures to prevent fresh alienation.

(iv) Provision of soil conservation measures and irrigation facilities in tribal areas ; and

(v) Strengthening of the agricultural credit system so as to provide for an appropriate agency adequate tribal representation to ensure easy facilities for both consumption and operational credit to tribals.

Redrawing of the Boundaries of Autonomous District Council Area

3.7 Tribal-majority villages which now fall outside the Autonomous District Council area and are contiguous to such area will be included in the Autonomous District and similarly placed non-tribal majority villages presently in the Autonomous District and on the periphery may be excluded.

Measures for Long-term Economic Development of Tripura

3.8 Maximum emphasis will be placed on extensive and intensive skill-formation of the tribal youths of Tripura so as to improve their prospects of employment including self-employment in various trades such as motor workshops, pharmacies, electronic goods, carpentry, tailoring, stationary, weaving, rice and oil mills, general stores, fishery, poultry, piggery, horticulture, handloom and handicrafts.

3.9 Special intensive recruitment drives will be organised for police and paramilitary forces in Tripura with a view to enlisting as many tribal youths as possible.

3.10 All India Radio will increase the duration and content of their programmes in tribal languages or dialects of Tripura. Additional transmitting stations will be provided for coverage even of the remote areas of the State.

3.11 The demands relating to self-employment of tribals, issue of permits for vehicles to tribals for commercial purposes, visits of tribal men and women to such places in the country as may be of value from the viewpoint of inspiration, training and experience in relevant fields will be considered sympathetically by the Government.

3.12 At least 2,500 Jhumia families will be rehabilitated in 5 centres or more in accordance with model schemes based on agriculture, horticulture, including vegetable growing, animal husbandary, fisheries and plantations, with a view to weaning them away from jhum cultivation. The scheme would also provide for housing assistance.

3.13 In the Autonomous District Council area of Tripura rice, salt and kerosene oil will be given at subsidised rates during lean months for a period of three years.

3.14 Conscious efforts will be made for effective implementation of the provisions of the Sixth Schedule to the Constitution in so far as it relates to Tripura.

1. (Bijoy Kumar Hrangkhawl)
2. (Anania Deb Barma)
3. (Kartik Kalal)
4. (Haripada Hrangkhawl)
5. (Utrenjoy Reang)
6. (Binoy Deb Barma)

On behalf of

Tripura National Volunteer

(P P. Shrivastav)
Additional Secretary
to the
Government of India
Ministry of Home Affairs

(I.P. Gupta)
Chief Secretary
to the
Government of Tripura

In the presence of

(General K.V. Krishra Rao,Retd.)
Governor of Tripura

(Sudhir Ranjan Majumdar)
Chief Minister of Tripura

Dated 12th August, 1988
Place: New Delhi

It is evident from the above Memorandum of Understanding that besides monetary compensation, the militants got a bunch of promises including reservation of 20 out of the 60 State Assembly seats for the tribals. Secondly, restoring the alienated lands for the tribals ; thirdly, employment scheme for tribal youth ; fourthly, more tribal radio programmes and fifthly, resettlement of 2,500 families which depend on shifting cultivation.

It is significant to note that the former General Secretary of the TUJS and second in rank in the present Congress-TUJS coalition Ministry, Nagendra Jamatia took the initiative in making contact with the TNV after the coalition formed Ministry took office. In support of this, Jamatia's observation may be made in this context. He says, "I took the initiative. Both the Chief Minister and I were involved in the spade-work. The actual negotiations were done by the Central Team but we were kept fully informed of all developments. Such secrecy was necessary".[15]

On the other hand Dasarath Deb, the veteran leader of the Communist movement in Tripura observes, "there is one element of mischief in the accord. That is, the promise not spelt out, of Chairmanship (for Bijoy) of a corporation connected with Tribal development. Our reading is that this will be linked to the programme of Jhumia rehabilitation Clause (3.12). This is at present within the jurisdiction of ADC, for the Jhumias live in ADC areas. The Sixth Schedule provision in this regard Clause 3(1) (b) are very clear. The proposal to entrust jhumia rehabilitation work to a corporation which may be headed by Bijoy is thus fraught with possibilities of tensions between the State Government and the ADC. The manoeuvering that has gone on with the accord suggests that moves to supersede the ADC cannot be ruled out."[16]

For Hrangkhawl, this was surely a come down. The TNV had presumably taken the path of insurgency and pitched its demand at the unrealisable 'Swadhin Tripura'. Even four months earlier, the list which was given out by Hrangkhawl contained the demands like Union Territory status for the Tribal districts, 50 per cent reservation of Assembly seats, introduction of inner line permits to restrict outsiders' entry and deportation of foreigners who came after 1965. In fact, the only political concession made in the pact was the promise to increase tribal representation in the State Assembly from the present 17 to 20. But this too is to take place not in the lifetime of the present House.[17] It is interesting to note that the present Assembly has already 19 tribal members. Two of these, Gaurishankar Reang (TUJS) and Kashiram Reang (Cong. I) were elected from two general seats, Santir bazar and Matabari respectively. These two constituencies on earlier occasions too had returned tribal candidate and along with Krishnanagar constituency of Agartala already stated to be declared reserved constituencies for the Scheduled Tribes. Of course, there are some unwritten understandings in the accord.

Hrangkhawl says, "It is all very simple and is related to the education and development of the tribal people. There are to be centres for providing training to tribal people to engage in business, and trades. For this there will be separate committees comprising representatives of the Government of India, the Government of Tripura and the TNV to monitor. We have asked for at least five thousand young tribal men and women to be provided training in different trades, in different parts of the country......There will be three or four such sub-committees to implement these schemes. Our representatives in these sub-committees will be our senior leaders. This I have explained to Srivastava (Union Additional Home Secretary) also. I said, "Look unless you give responsibility to my senior comrades......" All this is not on record ; it is one of those unwritten understandings."[18] But Shyamacharan Tripura, President of the Tripura Upajati Juba Samity is believed to be unhappy with the accord. According to him, "Bijoy has surrendered unconditionally. What he has got in the accord is less than what is contained in a tribal sub-plan. For instance, the tribals in Tripura are already getting subsidised rations for five months, during the lean period ; and the accord promises them three months of subsidised rations. He obviously did not know what he was signing. It is a complete sell out."[19]

Now it appears from the above background that the three parties viz , TNV, Central Government and State Government were in favour of party pact for some specific purposes The TNV President Bijoy Hrangkhawl was quite conscious of his weakness. He realised that time is running out and it will not be possible for him to fight from the jungles of Bangladesh any more. In fact he has been isolated in the tribal areas (due to highly politicised context of Tripura where the CPI(M) and the TUJS command the loyalty of most of the tribals).

Hence. It was an opportunity for Hrangkhawl to be in power. Moreover, he was given to understand that he will be made Chairman of the Tribal Jhumia Rehabilitation Corporation with Cabinet status. Naturally he thought that it would be wise to accept it. Whereas the Central and State Governments were interested in the hasty pact on the ground that Hrangkhawl came down to the lowest point which may not be possible in future. It is important to note that in this context with the TNV signing the peace accord, out of 437 of the activists 400 were absorbed in Government jobs, twenty three were recruited to the Assam Rifles while the rest got help in the self-employment scheme.[20] The TNV Chief, Hrangkhawl, however, sought economic help for about 5,000 more tribal youths, saying that though their names were not in the list submitted to the Government during negotiations they were active collaborators of his organization. Hrangkhawl, however, dispelled doubts about TNV's role in the State, saying: "There is no question of supporting the desperados as the days of insurgency in the North-East are over."[21]

But very recently, the growth of the Tripura National Liberation Front (TNLF)—a new underground tribal outfit, demanding a "Sovereign State of Tripura" has worried peoples of different circles of State. According to CPI(M)'s version: "The creation of new armed tribal extremist group in Tripura is the latest attempt of the coalition Ministry to destroy tribal bases of the CPI(M) and other democratic forces".[22] It has been also added that insurgency served the Congress(I)'s interests. It was well known that the TNV was used by the centre to unseat the Left Front Government in the State. A spokesman alleged that correspondence to this effect between Hrangkhawl and the then Mizoram Congress (I) President, Lalthanhawala had appeared in newspapers. It was the ruling combine's efforts at smashing the CPI(M)'s base among the tribals with the help of the army and paramilitary forces.[23] Thus, the creation of a new tribal outfit, was to achieve the purpose of the ruling front in Tripura. Whereas, the State Chief Minister and Home Minister and also the TUJS leaders would like to implicate the CPI(M) for complicity with the

TNLF. They have alleged that activists of the CPI(M)'s tribal front the Tripura Upajati Parishad are masquerading as TNLF volunteers and the CPI(M) is procuring arms from a neighbouring country to unsettle their coalition Government.[24] It is really strange that how an obscure outfit such as the TNLF could grow in strength so fast and indulge in killings, kidnappings, pillage and extortion in vast areas of the West and South Districts. The State Home Minister has said that the TNLF snatched at least 21 licensed guns from tribal villagers at Mandai which was the scene of the carnage of non-tribals in June, 1980.[25]

It is thus, evident that with the growth of the new underground tribal outfit, the intermittent rise of the insurgency which is directly related to land question as well as to the issue of ethnic problems poses a great problem in the State. Unfortunately, the authorities both at the Centre and in the State do not have a realistic policy to remove irritants in the Tripura's ethnic relations. Although, the peace accord had provisions for restoring alienated land and solving the problems of foreigners who had crossed over into the State after 1971 but continued migration from Bangladesh still keeps alive the reasons for insurgency in Tripura.

REFERENCES

1. Datta, S.: *The Telegraph*, 11th June, 1987.
2. Sarin, V.I.K.: *India's North-East in Flames*, New Delhi, 1980, p. 133.
3. *Ibid.*, p. 135.
4. *Ibid.*, p. 135.
5. *Ibid.*
6. *Tripura Darpan Saradiya*, 1391 B.E.
7. *Ibid.*
8. *The Front Line*, September 17-30, 1988.
9. *Paribartan*, 24-30 August, 1988 No. 8.
10. *Dinesh Singh Committee Report*, 1980.
11. *The Telegraph*, 15th May, 1987.
12. *Ibid.*

13. *India Today*, September 15, 1988.
14. *The Frontline*, September, 1988.
15. *Ibid.*
16. *Ibid.*
17. *Ibid.*
18. *Ibid.*
19. *Ibid.*
20. *The Statesman*, Thursday, July, 1989.
21. *Ibid,*
22. *Ibid.*
23. *Ibid.*
24. *Ibid.*
25. *Ibid.*

NINE

TASK AHEAD

From the discussions and findings made in the foregoing pages, it becomes evident that several factors-historic, demographic, ethnographic socio-economic and political have contributed to the cause of the tribal unrest in Tripura. It is, therefore, a scientific approach based in the light of our own and the other countrys' historic experience, is necessary for solving the tribal problems and also for uplifting the tribal people to bring them on a par with all other sections of the citizens of India.

Some authorities in the field of tribal studies have expressed the opinion that a sort of 'Reserve Land' or 'National Park' should be earmarked for the tribal people where they would be in a position to live freely in their own ways of life and thought. In other words, the tribal communities are to be kept segregated or isolated from the rest of the people. This is definitely a disastrous approach for the tribal peoples themselves. No tribe can survive in isolation or segregation. This becomes evident from the disappearance of many tribal communities from different parts of the World. Further, isolation or segregation can never further the cause of advancement and progress. Besides, this very policy runs counter to the provisions made in our Constitution which lays down that steps shall be taken for the advancement and progress of the tribal people. In this regard, Jawaharlal Nehru warned the nation at the time of inauguration of the 4th Gujjar Tribal Conference at Cholapur, of Dehradun during 1961 that : "We have to improve the nation as a whole. This line which demarcates as Scheduled Castes and Scheduled Tribes should be abolished."[1] Reference may also be made to Sardar Patel who was the Chairman of the Minority Advisory Committee at the time of framing the Constitution of India. He said, "In the long run, it would be in the interests of all to forget that there is anything like majority or minority in this country and to realise that in India there is only one community."[2] Thus, it is evident that our National leaders were fully alive to the tribal problems and accordingly specific provisions have been made in the Constitution itself for safeguarding the interests of the tribal people and also for making all our efforts for their advancement.

It is a fact that in accordance with the Constitutional provisions, both the Central and the State Governments have initiated and worked out many schemes and programmes for the upliftment and welfare of the tribal people. But unfortunately, all such schemes and their implementation by the Central and the State Governments have not yielded encouraging resuls. This was realised when a committee was appointed known as 'Dhebar Commission' in 1961 for making a comprehensive review of the work done by the State and the Central Government for the advancement of the tribal communities. The committee noted with regret the very slow progress of development and inadequate investment in the tribal areas. Even the measures taken for safeguarding the interests of the tribal peoples have been recorded as inadequate or insufficient.[3]

Besides the Dhebar Commission, several other commissions or committees were also formed from time to time to review the progress of the work done for the welfare are advancement of the tribal communities. One of such committees was headed by Shilu Ao Team.[4] According to this committee also cooperation has not made much headway in the tribal areas. Moreover, significant difference exists in the levels of technology and socio-economic organisations of the tribals and the larger society. Very recently, after the outburst of Mandai Massacre (1980) in Tripura, the Government of India constituted a committee consisting of seven members with Dinesh Singh, M.P. former Minister of External Affairs as Chairman. The Committee was asked to suggest measures for relief and rehabilitation of the victims of the violence, speedy restoration of normalcy and to bring about harmonious relations among the different sections of the population. The committee visited Tripura from 13th to 18th July, 1980. Its views and recommendation are given in Appendix II and III. This Committee also noted with regret that "the level and the rates of development of the two communities (Tribal and Non-tribal), practically in all respects, be it economic, cultural or educational, have been diverging. The conflict, therefore, is not confined to land only. It is a much bigger issue of the great economic, social and cultural divided between the two communities." The committee is also convinced "that the real solution to the problems of Tripura lies in the speedy development of this economically backward State, in the light of its resources and needs, and in a manner that ensures equitable distribution of the gains of development. The committee felt that despite a substantial rise in its per capital plan outlay during the last few years, Tripura has remained essentially backward in three major sectors ; agriculture, industry and transport."[5]

It is thus evident from various reports that the indifferent attitude of the Government and other sections of the people, the tribal communities of the State have been harbouring great discontent for a long time past which have been largely responsible for their violent outbursts at different times. So the crying need of the time is to safeguard the interests of the tribal communities and to make all our efforts to bring them shoulder to shoulder with other sections of the peoples of the State.

For this purpose, deliberate efforts are to be made for the integration of the tribal people within the larger section of the people of the State. Of course, such a policy of complete assimilation or the absorption of the tribal people within the fold of non-tribals is considered by some scholars as incompatible with the cultural pattern of India. It has been pointed out that the Indian society is composed of heterogenous cultures prevailing in different parts of the country. But despite the apparent diversity there is a keynote of cultural unity pervading all over the country. Naturally, it has been urged that there is hardly any need of complete assimilation of the tribal peoples and their culture. On the other hand, the tribal culture as such, in its various forms may thrive as one of the many segments of the totality of the Indian culture, and at the same time integration of the tribal people within the larger section is possible. It should be borne in mind that integration does not necessarily mean complete assimilation. In fact, such, integration will be made compatible with the heterogeneity of the Indian culture. If this policy is followed in the State of Tripura, it would imply that different tribal communities of the State shall be allowed to preserve their respective cultural distinctiveness as integral parts of the larger society of the State.

It is important to note that such type of integration of various component cultural elements within a particular nation has already been experimented in different parts of the World. The most classic example has been set by the Soviet Union, where all peoples with their respective cultural patterns have been integrated into a wholesome nation.[5] Reference may also be made of the United States of America and Switzerland where diverse cultural groups have been integrated into the nationhood. Thus, it would be wise that in the above perspectives of the works done by the Government and people of other countries of the World that the tribal problems of not only Tripura but also India as a whole are to be examined and solved for making them part and parcel of the Indian nation.

In Tripura, tribal's anger against the non-tribals is persisting even today. It is to be kept in mind that such feelings cannot be removed by the force of arms only. Actually speaking, anti-non-tribal feeling are the result of discontentments which have been mainly caused by the large scale economic exploitations carried out by some non-tribals specially Bengali Hindus. So the immediate burning problem is to put an end to all sorts of economic and other exploitations to which the tribal peoples of the State have been subjected to, for a long time past. In other words, all out efforts are to be made to cater to the primary needs of human existence, i.e. to remove hunger, nakedness, ignorance and some other superstitious beliefs and practices. Then only, ill-feelings against, which are being nourished and inflamed can be removed and both the tribals and the non-tribals can equally thrive as integrants of the great Indian nation. For this a scientific study of the problems faced by the tribals is necessary. It has already been stated the Jhuming' or shifting cultivation has been now found to be most uneconomic and less productive. So the Jhuming is to be replaced by plough cultivation or permanent agricultural operations. It may be borne in mind that the tribal peoples are now quite conscious of the benefits of the plough cultivation. But unfortunately, they have with the makes nor the available land for the same. naturally immediat provisions are to be made for the distrtion of avilable irrigated land, offering of financial assistar the purchase of bullocks, agricultural tools, crop seeds and also the every thing possible for safeguarding their interests by probiting money-lending or *dadan* system and also to not petmitting as traders and hants to carry on their hverse activites for the exploitation of the tribal peoples.

Again, to make agriculture in the kills paying, it has to be linked up with the systematic programmes for in which of new crops which would give ware economic return to the local people. Research seioars in the field also opine that the whole of N. E. Hilly region wherever jhuming is practised, is considered to by ideally suited for different horticultural crops. Fruit crops lihe citrus. banana, pineapple, guava are well adopted crops lower elevation situations, while temperate fruits like pear plum, apples are being tried successfully at higher altitude situations in addition differe vegetable crops, tuber crops like tapice (cassava), col case dioscorea, sweet potato and plantation crops like arecanut the pepper, coffee are also being cultivated successfully in merent agro-climatic zones of N.E.Hills. Scientific cultivation of these well adopted horticultural crops may become quite remunerative in Tripura and may very well be tried in Jhum land for improvement of the Jhumias.[6] It is, however, heartening to note that the experiments carried out by the soil conservation Department of the Government of Tripura have proved that the soil of Tripura Hills is very much suitable for rubber cultivation. It would be wise if rubber cultivation is made on commercial basis as the secondary aim and the primary aim being the economic development and rehabilitation of the tribal people of the hill areas as fast as possible.

Fortunately, rubber plantation in Tripura has already made its place and opened up a new horizon of economic development. Of course, it is also a fact that the North-Eastern Region lies well outside the traditional rubber belt but the existing agro-climatic conditions coupled with low elevation and other moderating influences has made areas within this region most suitable for rubber plantation. Experts are of opinion that average production of rubber in Tripura and in other areas of N.E. Region will be 1200 kg per hectare and if that is so, it may be added with full responsibility that a small grower having 1.5 hectare rubber plantation area under tapping will get 1800 kg of dry rubber worth of Rs. 24,000 at the current rate of market providing net income of Rs. 12,000 per annum after meeting the cost of maintenance and tapping and repayment of the Bank Loan.[7] Besides, rubber plantations would also provide fuel, wood, vegetable oil oil cakes and honey as by-products. Thus, according to rough calculation, the net income of a small rubber cultivator having 1.5 hectare rubber plantation are will get not less than Rs. 15,000 per annum i.e. monthly income from rubber plantation comes to Rs. 1250 whereas the average income of a jhumia household ranges between Rs. 1000 to Rs. 2000 per annum (A.F.C. Report) or on an average it is Rs. 1500 i.e. the monthly income being Rs. 250 only.[8]

It is also necessary that the sources of subsidiary income will have to be encouraged in order to improve the standard of living of the jhumias as well as to infuse into them the idea of permanent settlement and in this respect animal husbandry can be effectively introduced and popularised. Rotenhan (1966) referred to the importance of Animal Husbandry in Sukumland tribes in Tanzania as a best instance against economic and social risk.[9] The livestock protect them against uncertainties of rainfall and destruction of their crops by pests and plagues. It is interesting to note that these tribes prefer to store their earning in the form of cattle and not in grains. Similarly, certain tribes of Nagaland and Arunachal Pradesh consider possession of *Mithuns* as symbol of prestige and status. Most of the tribal families of Mizoram, Nagaland and also of Tripura rear pigs. Number of cattle, pig and poultry per hundred human population is larger in N.E. Region than the average of our country. Sixteen per cent of country's pig population and 3.6 per cent of poultry population is present only in N.E. Region (National Commission of Agriculture 1975).[10] Naturally, it may be pointed out that Animal Husbandry is one of the well suited practice which could be inducted to jhumias to supplement their economy. Depending on the land, classification for various uses and also on the availability of land, a unit of cattle or goat or pig or poultry or even mixed units may be reared by a family of jhumias. In the next phase, a slight modification or orientation may be needed for collection and sale of animal products like milk, butter, ghee, eggs and also for marketing mutton, pork, beef, birds etc.[11] It may be suggested that the State Government Veterinery and Animal Husbandry Department may assist in providing health guards for animals and other technical guidance. Now, it may rightly be presumed that once the animal unit is economically profitable, there will be no doubt that income from an Animal Husbandry will be a standing source of income for the jhumias besides meeting the domestic requirement of milk, meats, egg, etc.

In fact, Tripura's economic development cannot be viewed in isolation from that of the rest of the North-Eastern Region. Moreover, the States in the region are too small to undertake large economic-size industries separately. Therefore, scholars are of opinion that if they pool their resources, they may be able to get both efficient allocation and full utilisation of their resources. For this, the Industrial corporation can look into the possibilities of setting up of thermal and chemical complexes. Fortunately, the National Thermal Power Corporation (NTPC) is apparently satisfied with the infrastructural facilities for the setting up of a 500 MW super thermal project in Tripura with natural gas as its fuel.[12] According to official sources, the infrastructural bottleneck had once stood in the way of setting up of industries and now with the identification of huge natural gas and steady development of infrastructural facilities the State is now on the threshold of rapid industrialisation. In this context, it may be noted that the Dinesh Singh Committee (1980) rightly viewed that, "the setting up of a Regional Industrial Development Corporation could require support of institutional finance. Therefore, a North-Eastern Development Bank could be needed. This bank can be organised with capital from the Reserve Bank, Nationalised Banks and some other financial institutions."[13]

It may be noted again that all over the State of Tripura, deforestation has been causing a great concern. Tribal people largely dependent upon forest products have been thus deprived of their forest resources which have now become the primary concern of the contractors and the other exploiters. Accordingly strict legislative measures are to be taken for the protection of all forests with specific regulations regarding collection of forest produces, grazing ground, fire-wood collections etc. In other words, these provisions are to be made in such a way as not to jeopardise the interest of the tribal people in any manner. Besides, most of the forest products are now marketed by the State only through its agencies and contractors. This system is not compatible with the interest of the tribal people. In the fitness of things, it would be wise to form co-operatives in the rural areas for the collection, storage, transport etc., of all forest products. The State must deal directly with these tribal co-operative societies.

Tribesmen of Tripura are skilled craftsmen. They engage themselves in basket making, spinning and weaving. Here, the most widely practised craft is the manufacture of bamboo mats, baskets and manufacture of cloth from cotton dyed with indigenous vegetables. It is, therefore, necessary that the State should come forward to impart training on a scientific basis to the tribals through institutions established for the purpose. In the rural areas co-operative craft societies also may be formed so that all articles may be produced and marketed through them.

It may also be noted that it has been found that in the State of Tripura with its characteristic physical features bamboo is widely grown all over the territory. It has been estimated that 752 sq. miles of area are covered with Melocanna Bambusoides Trin in the valleys of Deo-Manu rivers.[14] Therefore, with such an enormous bamboo resources, a paper mill may be set up at Fatikroy in Kailashahar. The Dinesh Singh Committee also opines that with Tripura's enormous bamboo resources, the case for setting up a paper mill is very strong. A feasibility report for setting up this plant at Fatikroy in Kailashahar sub-division, has already been completed. The committee strongly recommends the setting up of the paper plant as it will lead to large direct and indirect employment and massive development of the forestry sector. Besides meeting the needs of the paper mill, social conservation and ecology also demand proper development of the forestry sector.[15]

Ignorance breeds distrust, it is therefore, essential that if the tribal peoples are to be placed on a par with other sections of the Indian nation, the primary need is the removal of illiteracy. This is possible only by imparting formal education in conformity with the tribal ways of life and thought. For this purpose, what is needed most is the establishment of primary education all over the rural areas. The spread of education must be through the medium of 'Kak-barak' i.e. tribal language and regional language may be placed in the next stage of educational programme. As to tribal language a clear cut policy has been adopted by the Central Government. This would be evident from the observation made by Nehru in 1952: "It is absolutely clear to me that Government must encourage the tribal languages. It is not enough simply to allow them to prevail. They must be given all possible support, and the conditions in which they can flourish must be safeguarded. Accordingly every effort is to be made to encourage the development of tribal languages and this is possible only if the formal education is imparted through the mother tongue of the people concerned. But the trouble is that generally, tribal peoples did not have their own script. This is the initial difficulty in the development of any language. Recently, however, some tribals have been demanding a separate script of their own for writing down their own language.

In this respect, a section of the tribal people is in favour of introducing 'Ol Chiki' script which has been found and systematised for the tribal languages by Raghunath Murmu of Orissa. On the other hand Christian Missionaries have been encouraging the tribal peoples to adopt the Roman Script. In Tripura as well, some tribal Christian converts have raised a cry for the adoption of the Roman script for the Kak-barak language of Tripura. But scholars are of the opinion that there is little justification for the adoption of Roman script because such script is not in conformity with the country's traditional languages and methods of writings. Currently the arguments go in favour of the adoption of the Devanagri script which is the mother script of various Indian languages. Hence, for all practical purposes, Devanagri script may be adopted, because it would place the tribal people more in touch with other peoples of India and also their languages.

Now, for the removal of illiteracy and imparting of formal education, a chain of primary schools is immediately called for. But it is to be kept in mind that such schools are to be manned by tribal teachers and the medium of schooling must be Kak-barak only. At the initial stage, there may be difficulties to find sufficient number of qualified tribal persons to man such institutions. So in the absence of qualified teaching personnel amongst the tribals, the non-tribals may be appointed in the beginning. In such a case, however, particular emphasis is to be laid, while selecting the non-tribal teachers, on the question of their familiarity and deep acquaintances with the tribal language and life pattern as a whole. Above all, such non-tribal teachers must possess a high regard or respect for the tribal ways of life and thought. As regards course contents or the syllabi, attention should be directed towards knowledge about the surrounding landscape and socio-economic life patterns including recreations and some basic ideas relating to the country and nation as a whole. In short, the primary educational programme is not to be divorced from the traditional tribal-life pattern and at the same time it ought to be engrained with all matters of national integration and cohesion.

Tripura is geographically isolated. The only opening to the rest of India by land being through Assam and Mizoram on North and North-east covering an area of 162 km.[16] Thus the wide communication gap between the inhabitants of the State of Tripura and their compatriots in the rest of India is equally responsible for misunderstandings about the motives, beliefs and traditions of the different ethnic-linguistic groups. The only link again is subjected to frequent disruption by heavy rains and chronic floods. As a matter of fact, such geographical isolation has given rise to "mutually antagonistic and fiercely parochial cultures."

Every effort is to be made for the improvement of physical communications by the construction of roads and pathways, so that regular communications may be made possible from village to village. There are many hurdles no doubt because the tribal peoples are particularly settled on hill tops and forest areas. It may not be wholly possible, but every attempt is to be made for providing communication facilities in such a way as to make all the isolated pockets accessible. Again, for the removal of socio-economic communication gap, the State Government should organise weekly and bi-weekly markets in such a way as to enable all the neighbouring peoples to attend and communicate with one another. Such a market would be the best media for communication between the tribals and the non-tribals as well, because it is here, that people of both the communities meet together and discuss all matters affecting their life and activities. Further, in such place arrangements may be made for visual education through film-shows projectors etc. Along with these, attention may be made to organise sports, amusements for the recreation of the tribal peoples. These are to be done frequently in such a way as the tribal people would think that they are not at all divorced from the rest of the Indian society.

North-Eastern Council

The need of the hour is full-blooded development of the State. There are two purposes. First, the socio-economic upliftment of the tribal people. Second, the integration of the tribal people with the larger section of the people of the State and of the country. It is encouraging to note that the North-Eastern Council (NEC) which was inaugurated in 1971, provided the necessary organizational set up for co-ordinated development of the region. The task of the council is to draw attention to the much neglected work and provide funds for it, help and promote co-ordination of development in the different units of the region. Critics, however, doubt about the bonafides of New Delhi in setting up this council. Sarin (1980) observes: The suspicion was that the council was designed in some way to reduce the power of the States in the region and to impose upon them the will of the Centre.[17] Indira Gandhi, however, in her inaugural speech wisely disabused the mind of the people saying that the Council was neither the thin end of the wedge of Central interference nor a super Government to surpervise the work of the different administrations in the area. She emphasised that Co-operation does not in any way lessen the authority of individual Governments. Not only that, over the years, the right of the constituent units to draw up their own State plans has remained unimpaired nor has there been any attempt to limit their scope. The regional plans only supplement the State plans and are financed entirely by the Centre. Financial assistance made available to the units is not reduced on this account.[18]

The Council initiated the beginning of a new integration after the centrifugal forces had run their legitimate course. Since its inception the Council has frequently discussed matters in which some or all the units had common interest and advised both the Union Government and the Constituent States concerned as to the action to be taken on any such matter, particularly relating to economic and social planning.[19]

It is true that the Central subsidies to help this backward region to catch up with the main stream cannot be decried but at the same time it is to be kept in mind that the cause of backwardness and its nature are different in different societies. J.K. Galbraith in his 'Economic Development in Perspective' observed : We must recognise that economic development is a process-one that extends, in range from new nations of Africa but slightly removed from their tribal structure to the elaborate economic and social apparatus of Western nations. At each stage along with this contention there is an appropriate policy for further advance. What is appropriate at one stage is wrong at another.[20] He also emphasised that the ability to use capital in any considerable volume is itself the result of development : If it is available before the condition for its use are available, it will be ineffectively employed or possibly wasted.[21] Naturally, mere inflow of Central subsidies from New Delhi without overall socio-technological development planning, the purpose will cease to have its significance. Or in other words in a vast area like North-eastern region having different economic and cultural characteristics, one centralised plan uniformly drawn for the entire region may not be the best method of attaining the objective of rapid economic growth and other social objectives. Naturally, the welfare programmes should be decentralised and as such, work should now be entrusted to the respective Panchayats in order to avoid duplicacy and also to avoid infiltration of non-tribals who enjoy no confidence of the concerned people. This will ensure decentralisation and at the same time it is necessary in the interest of democratic planning and integration as advised by Dhebar Commission in his report on Scheduled castes and Scheduled Tribes.[22]

As regards the second purpose for undertaking and implementing tribal welfare measures, that is, the integration of the tribal people with the larger section of the people of the State and of the country it may be pointed out that the question of integration of the tribal people cannot be solved simply by carrying out welfare measures or some other steps by any State or ruling authority. Integration cannot be achieved by giving incentives alone. It has a law of its own. It is through a natural process that integration becomes a reality. In this connection, a reference may be made to the lesson that

ent time onwards. It is qulte well known that India is the home *par excellence* of innumerable tribes belonging to diverse ethnic and cultural groups. Many of these tribes even came from outside under different texts and circumstances and got themselves settled on the soil of India. But all these tribal peoples have been either completely assimilated or integrated within the vast area of the culture rather Hindu culture. According to Risley (1901) "all over India at the present moment tribes are gradually and intensively being transformed into castes.[23] It is thus evident from historical background that there was no deliberate efforts or attempts on the part of the Government or the King to Hinduise the tribal people. On the other hand, the tribals, voluntarily entered into the Hindu fold and accepted Hinduism. This they probably did or are doing because of the very fact that they enjoyed or enjoy complete liberty in maintaining their own traditions and culture and also in pursuing their own respective occupations. In reality, there was hardly any interference whatsoever. The diverse tribal groups have been persisting even today as belonging to so many low caste orders within the large framework of the Hindu fold. This kind of integration achieved without any deliberate efforts whatsoever excepting a little initiative taken by the torch-bearers of the Brahmanical culture.

Again, a perusal of the ancient Indian literary texts more particularly the *Dharmasastras* and other connected literature reveals that many tribal groups were completely assimilated and they have been assigned various caste orders in accordance with occupations pursued by them or scheduled for them. That they have been recognised as fully assimilated would be apparent from the fact that even the *Sastrakaras* have traced their respective origins from unions between members of the opposite sex belonging to one or the other of the four traditional *Brahmanical* caste orders. A critical examination also reveals that even some of the caste groups which now occupy a higher social position, of course outside the four traditional social orders in the Brahmanical hierarchy, appear to have tribal origin, but their absorption has become so complete that no trace of their tribes origin can be found at present.

It is thus evident from the above analysis that in the process of assimilation ruling authority had little role to play. But it happened in the natural course which may rightly be called historical force or circumstances.

As for example in Tripura, the historical process towards the integration of the tribal people within the Hindu fold appear to have been quite active for a long time past through close cultural contact with the Bengali Hindus. It has been seen that both the tribals and the non-tribals have most successfuly made mutual cultural adjustments amongst them. The implication is that the path for integration has been largely smoothened and made easy for the adoption of certain concrete steps towards integrating the tribal peoples as segments of the great Indian nation.

REFERENCES

1. Bharadwaj, A.N. : *The Problems of Scheduled Castes and Scheduled Tribes in India,* Delhi, 1979.
2, *Bombuy Chronicle,* 26th May, 1949.
3. *National Committee Report on Development of Tribal Areas,* New Delhi, 1961.
4. Roy Burman, B.K.: *The Tribal People of India,* Publications Division Government of India. New Delhi, 1973, p. 182.
5. *The Dinesh Singh Committee Report,* 1980.
6. Datta, Majumdar : *The Tribal People of India.*
7. Borthakur, D.N., Awasthi, R.P., Ghosh, S.P. : *Alternative System of Farming for Increasing Productivity in Jhum lands,* Published in *the Shifting Cultivation in N.E.,* India, 1976, Shillong, p. 63.
8. A brief note by the Tripura Rubber Plantation Corporation Ltd., (Manuscript).
9. *Ibid.*
10. Roy, D.J. and Verma ; (*I.C.A.R. Research Complex for N.E. Hills Region*) *Shifting cultivation in North East India,* Shillong, 1976, p. 48.
11. *Ibid.*
12. *Ibid.*
13. *The Telegraph,* 25th August, 1989.
14, *The Dinesh Singh Committee Report* 1980.
15. Ganguly, J.B. : *Economic Problems of the Jhumias of Tripura,* 1968, p. 19.
16. *The Dinesh Singh Committee Report,* 1980.

17. Roy Burman, B.K. : *The Demographic and Socio-economic Profile of the Hill Areas of N.E. India*, 1970, p. 140.
18. Sarin, V.I.K.: *India's North East in Flames* New Delhi, 1980, pp. 188-189.
19. *Ibid.*,
20. Galbraith, J.K. : Economic Development in perspective United States information Service, New Delhi.
21. *Ibid.*,
22. Bharadwaj A.N. : *The Problems of Scheduled Castes and Scheduled Tribes in India*, New Delhi, 1979, p. 82.
23. Risley, H.H : *The People of India*, London, 1915, pp. 72-76.

APPENDIX—I

* STATEMENT SHOWING TRIBAL POPULATION, GAON SABHAS AND REVENUE VILLAGES OF TRIPURA TRIBAL AREAS DISTRICT.

1.	Total Population 6,33,322		
	S.T. Population ...	+	4,52,809
	S.C. Population ...	+	38,660
	Other Population ...	+	1,41,853
		Total	6,33,322
2.	Total Gaon Sabhas within the Autonomous District	—	330
3.	Total Revenue villages	—	462
4.	Area	—	7132.56 sq. km.

* Tripura Tribal Areas District Office of the Chief Executive Officer, Swet Mahal, Agartala.
Ref. No. F. 11(18)/ADC/82.

APPENDIX—II

STATEMENT SHOWING DEATHS, INJURED, LOSS OF PROPERTY ETC. DURING MANDAI MASSACRE (JUNE, 1980).

1.	No. of Deaths ...	539
	(i) Non-tribal ...	323
	(ii) Tribal ...	69
	(iii) Unidentified ...	145
	(iv) Policemen on duty ...	1
	(v) Policemen off duty ...	1
2.	No. of Injured ...	601
	(i) Non-tribal ...	535
	(ii) Tribal ...	66
3.	No. of Persons arrested ...	1621
4.	No. of Fire arms seized ...	132
5.	No. of Police Stations affected	19
6.	No. of Villages affected	156
7.	No. of Paras (Hamlets) affected	519
8.	No. of Panchayat ...	150 (out of 689)
9.	No. of Refugee camps ...	138 (Tribals-45)
10.	No. of Refugees in camps ..	1,89,919 (Tribal 40,160)
11.	No. of Refugees who had left the camps	1,17,789 (Tribal 17,473)

12. Population affected : Tribal-1,44,549 & others
2,27,499
13. Cultivable land affected ; 1,86,957'52 acres.
14. No. of Huts gutted : 34,661, Tribal-11025.
15. No. of Missing : 1811, Tribal-443.
16. Loss of property : Tribal- Rs. 4,43,53,127.
Non-tribal- Rs. 16,43,78,757.

Total...... Rs. 20,91,63,014.

---

* The above report was given by the State Government to the Dinesh Singh Committee in 1980.

APPENDIX—III

RECOMMENDATIONS OF THE DINESH SINGH COMMITTEE (8TH JULY, 1980)

The Government of India in the Ministry of Home Affairs constituted a Committee on 8.7.80 after Mandai Massacre (June, 1980) with the following :

1. Sri Dinesh Singh, M.P. ... Chairman
   (Former Minister of External Affairs)
2. Sri J.D. Sethi ... ... Member
   (Former Member with Planning Commission)
3. Sri V.K.C. Deo, M.P. ... Member
4. Sri K.B. Deb Burman ... Member
   (M.P., Former Maharaja of Tripura)
5. Sri A.N. Banerjee ... ... Member
   (Retired Secretary, Ministry of Works and Housing).
6. Sri J.D.O. Souza.
7. Sri P.S. Raturi.

The Committee visited Tripura from 13th to 18th July, 1980. After its return to Delhi on the 18th July 1980, the Committee held various meetings to consider crystalise and finalise its views. The recommendations of the Committee are as follows :

Recommendations

7.1 The basic problems of Tripura, as that of the North eastern regions as a whole, is the lack of understanding of the real requirements of the tribals and of making them as integral part of the national life. Conscious efforts made towards development undertaken after independence have, unfortunately, not been able to bridge the emotional gap. There has been more emphasis on their material and political development and less on psychological and cultural integration.

7.2 The need is for the psycho-cultural, economic and political integration of the tribal people with the development in the rest of the country. During the colonial rule the tribal areas were largely untouched and isolated from the rest of the country. The entry of outsiders was strictly restricted and the tribals were left to manage their own affairs. With the advent of independence and with the improvement of communications, the traders, new politically oriented missionaries and the land grabbers made inroads into the tribal society. The problem was compounded by a large influx of refugees from East Pakistan (now Bangladesh). In Tripura, it even changed the demographic situation against the tribals. The tribals no longer feel secure in their home and are fearful of their domination and exploitation in every respect. It is patent that the tribals cannot be kept isolated, nor would they wish to be so. To keep them isolated would frustrate all efforts towards integration, at the same time they must have greater say in their affairs. The immediate need is, therefore, to prepare the tribals to face the challenges of the new industrial society and the technological age in which the country has entered.

7.3. Keeping in view, the requirements of a long term perspective the prime need is for the proper type of education to prepare them to meet the future without losing their mooring to play a greater role in the management of their affairs and the same time to appropriate the benefits of association in the Indian Union.

7.4. Coming to the recent events, Tripura has a traumatic experience in the last few weeks. Recovery from that trauma will, naturally need, time, but must not be left to mere passage of time. There is a great deal that can and must be done to hasten the process of recovery by a speedy rehabilitation of the sufferers, by the restoration of harmony between the two major groups, by the protection of tribal interests and above all, by the acceleration of pace of economic growth of the State with an equitable distribution of fruits thereof.

7.5. The mutal loss of confidence and apprehensive about the alleged partisan role of the administration that was felt in the wake of violence necessitates a political approach to the solution of the problem. This approach would require that, in the immediate short run, a Citizens' Relief and Rehabilitation Committee under the Chairmanship of the Chief Minister and involving a really wide spectrum of community leadership as well as political groups, should be constituted to supervise the work of relief and rehabilitation. The Committee must be such as will not only restore immediate political confidence among them who have been affected but also among the public at large.

It would also assist in the creation of atmosphere the resumption, without fear, of general political activities in the State.

7.6. The normal distribution system for committee has been disrupted and has yet to be restored. It should be the function of the relief committee to see that in areas where neither private nor public distribution system exists, some adhoc arrangements be made on high priority to take the essential commodities to these areas.

7.7. The pace of rehabilitation needs to be speeded up. Groups of refugees should individually be escorted to their villages to attend to their delayed agricultural operations and to rebuild their houses. To discourage new entrants in the relief camps, it should be announced that rehabilitation benefits will be available only to those who were identified as sufferers.

7.8. The Central Government is giving generous relief assistance to the State and is expected to give additional Plan funds. It is advisable that a careful supervision and monitoring of the distribution and effective utilisation of funds/materials be made by a monitoring group that should include

Officers from the State as well as representatives of the Central Government. To expedite transfer of funds and actual decisions in respect of the use of these funds, as well as for their proper use, it is recommended that the Central Government should appoint a Liason officer to the State Government and he should remain there until such time as the State is brought back to normalcy.

7.9. A per-requisite for the return to normalcy and restoration of confidence among all groups is the visible presence of the Police and security forces in the State. It is necessary to ensure that stray incidents do not get inflamed into major conflicts, nor do reprisals take place, particularly against the tribals.

7.10. The committee is of the view that State forces in Tripura need to be reorganised and better trained. Their intelligence set up also deserves considerable improvement. The State forces should be reinforced by the presence of the Central Police Forces in reasonable strength. Vigorous patrolling on the affected areas and of potential trouble spots should continue for sometime more.

7.11. The committee is of the view that although the presence of the army has greatly helped in restoring confidence among the communities, it would be undesirable to use the army for police work and it may be replaced by the Central Police Force as soon as possible.

7.12. Fears were expressed by many people before the Committee about partisan character and functioning of the administration. It would be desirable on the part of the State Government of resotre the apprehensions and tone up the administration wherever necessary.

7.13. Much of the tension between the two communities arises from the tribals apprehensions that they are losing their land and that they are being exploited by others. On the other hand, the apprehension of the Bengalees are that they would be uprooted for the second time as a result of the State going to be permanently divided into two separate hostile blocs of two communities by the operation of the Autonomous District Council Act. The Committee, therefore, very strongly recommended that the problems arising out of the respective fears of the two communities should not be viewed in isolation, these are two sides of the same problem. The restoration of land to the tribals should not be delayed any longer and this measure should be immediately accompanied by full and complete rehabilitation of non-tribals from whom land is taken away.

7.14. Conscious and visible efforts must be made to reduce the glaring disparity in the economic conditions between the two communities. In the final analysis, the solution to this problem lies in the acceleration of Tripura's economic development for which short term measures have been suggested at some length in Chapter four. Long term normalcy and harmony would depend upon the rate of economic development and equitable distribution of its benefits to the people.

7.15. Short term measures are summerised below :

(a) The Committee recommends that in view of the disruption of the proposed arrangements for Autonomous District Council of Tribal Planning and Implementation Advisory Committee be appointed to review all plans for economic and social development of the tribal areas. This Committee will be presided over by the Chief Minister and will include all the tribal M.L.As, technical and other suitable persons.

(b) The State's demand for additional plan outlay of about 4.8 crore of which about 3 crores would be transferred to the tribal sub-plan, should be examined sympathetically by the Planning Commissioner.

(c) To provide both consumption and capital credit to the farmers, especially to the tribals, Co-operative Banking should be pressed into service. Nationalised Banks should open more branches in Tripura as the State is not adequately served by the Banking system.

(d) The organisational structure of the Integrated Tribal Development Projects (ITDP), there of which have been set up so far, should be extended to all the tribal areas. ITDP can become the nucleus for the devolution of power.

(e) Tripura should get equal to last year's allotment of about 30,000 tonnes of food-grains for its Food for Work to employ those who have been temporarily dislocated.

7.16. In the long term Tripura's economic development cannot be viewed in isolation from that of the rest of the N.E. Region—the N.E. Council has, therefore, to play an increasing role in planning for development on a regional basis. Since it is NEC's limited budgetory resources that put serious constraints on its role of regional planning, its budgetory base should be enlarged.

7.17. NER's economic development has been retarded by lack of adequate transport and marketing facilities. Tripura has suffered more than any other State, largely because of historical reasons. The State nominally has a rail-head. The feasibility of extending the railway system into the State needs to be explored.

Meanwhile, a really large road building programme should be given a high priority. The Committee supports the recommendation of the National Transport Policy Committee that the region needs "short haul air service" and that Kamalpur and Kailashahar in Tripura should have air links. Again the Indian Airlines and the proposed third level air services should be persuaded to use their spare capacity to transport fresh produce, particularly fruits at concessional rates to market in Calcutta. Similar rail-freight concessions should also, be necessary.

7.18. The idea of N.E. Industrial Corporation should also be seriously examined. This corporation could be especially responsible for industrial planning on the basis of local materials and resources. It could handle the supply of industrial raw materials at the regional level. It could also assist the State Government in obtaining other material inputs like cement and steel required for the development of basic infrastructure. To speed up the work of this Regional Industrial Development Corporation, a N.E. Development Bank should be set up to provide necessary institutional finance.

the proposal to set up a Paper Mill in Tripura which may cost up to Rs. 200 crores.

7.19. In the agricultural sector, Tripura's future lies in the utilisation and development of the undulating uplands. Therefore, a special cropping programme needs to be devised for three areas. The State has considerable potential for the development of tea, jute and rubber etc. There is also an enormous need and scope for development of sericulture which could be used to resettle landless farmers, specially tribal Jhumias.

7.20. Next to paddy cultivation, horticulture is the most important source of generating new employment and income. So far efforts have been concentrated on the cultivation of pineapple only. The facilities available with the Tripura Small Industries Corporation for pineapple processing are inadequate. The Central Food Technological Research Institute's Rs. 1.2 Crores scheme needs early consideration.

7.21. With Tripura's enormous bamboo resources, the case for setting up a Paper Mill is very strong. A feasibility report for setting up this plant at Fatikroy in Kailasahar sub-division has already been completed. The Committee strongly recommends the setting up of the Paper Plant as it will lead to large direct and indirect employment and massive development of the forestry sector. Besides, meeting the needs of the Paper Mill, Social conservation and ecology also demand proper development of the forestry sector.

7.22. Social integration is the main problem. Within the State, education will play a crucial role in promoting integration and therefore needs to be specially attended to. In the field of education, the Central Government should step-up education and cultural activities which will give the tribal people a concrete picture of gains of their wider associations with the rest of the country and make them feel that they are equal partners in development as also in sharing the obligations. It will also be necessary to establish special schools run by the Central Government started by socially trained local teachers, preferably tribals in the tribal areas on a fairly wide scale. The heads of these schools should be carefully selected for their dedications to the cause of education and integrations

The curriculars should be suitably altered to impart an integrated education. In this connection three points may have to be kept in view. First, the staff should be local so that they do not have to worry about families far away, and especially trained for the purpose. Secondly, the curricular should take into account the needs of the community in which their school is situated, while integrating it with the educational system prevailing in the country. Thirdly, maximam emphasis should be placed on extensive and intensive skill formation of the younger generation so as to improve their prospects of self-employment.

7.23. The State Government could be well advised to pay greater attention to the representation of tribals in the Civil Services, which is today below their proportion to the population.

7.24. To counter the feeling of isolation from the national mainstream, the committee thinks it necessary that All India Radio should give much greater attention and coverage to the people of the State, particularly the tribals. A high power transmitter should be set up in a place from where it can reach all the people of the N.E. Region. Powers of existing transmitters should also be increased and more transmitting stations should be set up at appropriate locations.

7.25. Finally, we recognise that neither peace nor harmony will return unless the leaders of public opinion in the State and elsewhere desire it, that desire must be sufficiently strong to restrain a temptation to secure partisan advantage out of June disaster. The people's agony should not provide an opportunity for petty political gains.

INDEX